Rafts, Raccoons, & Revelations

"Reading Pete Griffin's *Rafts, Raccoons and Revelations: Growing Up on a Great Lake* feels like a bracing dip into the waters he describes so vividly. He brings an adult sensibility and understanding to the mishaps and enthusiasms of his younger self. Whether helping his mother-in-law land a King Salmon or setting sail with his sister Terrie on a raft built for two, Pete's love for the people and places who formed him shines in every story. **It's a heartfelt tribute** to hard-working, thoroughly human people living in a wild and wonderful place."

—**Anne Rutherford,** Storyteller, teaching artist, author

"In this book, self-deprecating **naturalist Pete Griffin** takes us through his free-range youth with aplomb, respectfully handling sometimes dire situations with humor and humanity. While young Pete is given chances to make bad decisions, his familial and acquainted family are always close by to guide him through challenges. This book lets us follow Griffin as he navigates the natural and interpersonal worlds. We may not recognize the situations, but we can connect to the lessons. **I laughed, almost cried."**

—**Norm Brecke,** storyteller, teacher, and author

"Pete's engaging style of illustrating a scene through stories, he here thoughtfully chronicles experiences gained and lessons learned while growing up on the shores of northern Lake Huron. Pete has a gift for learning through life experiences and then teaching through the stories that those experiences inspire. Whether taking account of catching mayflies, starting a first job, or guiding a fishing adventure, I found myself immersed in the stories and inspired to apply Pete's values of learning and teaching to my own life.

—**Kevin St. Onge,** STEM (Science, Technology, Engineering, and Math) educator

"Pete Griffin's newest book—*Rafts, Raccoons, and Revelations*—is a revelation itself. Full of tall tales and small tales of his growing up years in the Upper Peninsula of Michigan, this book's pages are love letters to the people who shaped him as a naturalist, biologist, friend, son, husband, and storyteller. From the lakeshore towns of Cedarville and Hessel to the king salmon-laden waters of Alaska, **Griffin throws out his lines and hooks us, reeling us in**—sometimes slowly, sometimes swiftly—until we lie flopping at his feet in stunned appreciation and joy. Secrets are kept and revealed, and the heart is laid open in all its complexity, humor, and humanity.

Here is my advice—buy this book, take it down to the dock with you, sit with your feet in the water, and let Pete Griffin instruct you how, as Thoreau said, to go to the wilderness (of trees and water and love) "as a hungry man to a crust of bread."

    —Martin Achatz, two-time Poet Laureate of the Upper Peninsula

"In childhood, we are intrigued with the idea of building a raft and sailing away from the familiarity of home and parents. **In the spirit of Huck Finn, Pete Griffin** welcomes you to a time when kids learned by doing, undoing, and doing again. Experience Pete's free-range childhood in a time when if he wanted something, he had to design and build it himself, sometimes with a little help from his sister, Terrie. Join Pete and a cast of eccentric characters from his childhood in the Les Cheneaux Islands of Michigan's Upper Peninsula. Pete invites you to inhabit a simpler time. **He guides us through explorations** of woods, waters, critters, mentors, and clever inventions of all kinds. This delightful read is filled with nature's metaphors for growth, development, caring for each other, and caring for our beautiful natural world. Along the way, Pete shares real family challenges and some real hard times that helped shape him."

    —Robin Nott, Shady Grove Storytelling, Kalamazoo, Michigan

Rafts, Raccoons, & Revelations

Growing Up on a Great Lake

Pete Griffin

The Storytelling Forest Ranger

Parkhurst Brothers Publishers

MARION, MICHIGAN

www.parkhurstbrothers.com
Consumers may order Parkhurst Brothers books from their favorite online or bricks-and-mortar booksellers, expecting prompt delivery. Parkhurst Brothers books are distributed to the trade through the Chicago Distribution Center. Trade and library orders may be placed through Ingram Book Company, Baker & Taylor, Follett Library Resources and other book industry wholesalers. To order from Chicago Distribution Center, phone 1-800-621-2736 or fax to 800-621-8476. Copies of this and other Parkhurst Brothers Publishers titles are available to organizations and corporations for purchase in quantity by contacting Special Sales Department at our home office location, listed on our web site. Manuscript submission guidelines for this publishing company are available at our web site.

Printed in the United States of America
First Edition, October 2021
Printing history: 2021 2022 2022 2023   8 7 6 5 4 3 2 1
Library Cataloging Data
    1.   Author–Peter Griffin, American storyteller, and author
    2.   Subject–Nonfiction, Americana
    3.   Subject–Memoir
    2021-trade paperback and e-book

ISBN: Trade Paperback   978162491-169-9
ISBN: e-book   978162491-170-5

Parkhurst Brothers Publishers believes that the free and open exchange of ideas is essential for the maintenance of our freedoms. We support the First Amendment of the United States Constitution and encourage all citizens to study all sides of public policy questions, making up their own minds.

Cover and interior design by   Linda D. Parkhurst, Ph.D.
Acquired for Parkhurst Brothers Publishers by   Ted Parkhurst
Proofread by   Richard Culbertson
     102021

Dedication

I DEDICATE THIS BOOK TO THE THREE MOST INFLUENTIAL PEOPLE IN MY LIFE. I am forever indebted to my wife, Kathryn. While our lives overlapped at Lake Superior State College in Dr. B.E. Smith's General Ecology class, we did not formally meet until we both had summer jobs with the US Forest Service in the summer of 1973. You will find that story (Let's Go Fishing) at the end of this collection.

She has supported me in my pursuit of career advancement, as we uprooted ourselves three times; Cadillac, Michigan to Walker, Minnesota; Walker to Ketchikan, Alaska; and finally, Ketchikan to Juneau, Alaska. She stuck with me and encouraged me. I am a far better person for her influence.

I am indebted, as well, to our children, Peter and Meg. Moving across country to unknown places, having to make new friends can be terribly difficult. With them, I have experienced love far beyond what I knew possible before parenthood. I am fortunate to have them in my life.

This is also dedicated to my parents, Pete and Aldyth, who, each in their own way, prepared me for the future: teaching me always to give more than expected, be independent, and maintain a sense of humor.

Acknowledgments

It takes a village to raise a storyteller, or something to that effect. For all the people with whom I grew up in the Les Cheneaux, my friends, my classmates, and my mentors, I thank you.

A very big thank you is due my sister, Terrie, an integral part of my childhood. She has often asked of me: "Do you remember ...?" which often led to details in these stories that I'd long forgotten. Terrie, when you write your own book disputing every story within, please remember to be kind!

I owe a debt of gratitude to my editors and publishers, Ted and Linda Parkhurst. Ted took years to gently coax a manuscript from me. Linda provided graphic arts skills to design a memorable cover. Thank you, both.

In 2014, I attended a National Storytelling Network Conference workshop led by Sean Buvala. His workshop opened my eyes to the idea that storytellers can, and should, write books. His encouragement and his coaching helped lead me to this point. Thank you, my friend.

The following storytellers are some of many who have inspired me through their workshops, their coaching, and their performances over the years: Connie Regan-Blake, Jay O'Callahan, Kim Weitkamp, Steven Henegar, Judy Sima, Kevin Cordi,

Jim May, Loren Niemi, Jo Radner, and Ward Rubrecht. Thank you, all.

To Robin Nott, Greg Weiss, Kevin St. Onge, Martin Achatz, Norm Brecke, Anne Rutherford, and Rebecca Glotfelty: I am humbled that you all graciously provided early reviews of my manuscript. Thank you so much!

Contents

Foreword

IN THE FALL OF 1970, I BEGAN ATTENDING COLLEGE at what was then Lake Superior State College (ahem, now a *university*). I intended to qualify eventually for jobs as a fish or wildlife biologist, which I thought would allow me to work in the woods all day long without ever having to talk to another human being.

I had been a straight A student at Cedarville High School and was graduated with a grade point average somewhere near three point nine on a four point scale. That wasn't enough to rank as either Valedictorian or Salutatorian as there were three young women in our Senior Class with GPAs much closer to four point than mine. College would be a snap, I figured. I had a full-tuition scholarship from the State of Michigan and a $300/year scholarship from an Eastern Upper Peninsula foundation.

In high school, I didn't study other than a little reading in study hall. I had a gift for taking tests.

As a college freshman, I was surprised just how difficult college was. High school had not prepared me for the demands of college academics. In my new life, studying between classes was critical.

My first two years at Lake Superior State consisted of a series of lessons in the importance of pre-class preparation. When a photograph of Norm, a Class of '69 Cedarville graduate, was featured on a Lake Superior State program touting outdoor careers available with a two-year Associates Degree in

Natural Resources Technology, I considered dropping out of the four-year Bachelor of Science program. It looked like Norm was having the kind of fun that I was not. Luckily, after consulting my instructors in the Biology Department, I did not change my program.

In my third year, I was determined to do better. The back row of the class was where I had lived my first two years. Realizing a challenge reading the instructor's blackboard diagrams, I moved to the front row. Now outfitted with glasses ("College myopia," the optometrist said, "a common condition"), my notes more accurately reflected what I needed to understand.

With most of the mandatory required classes out of the way, I began doing better in biology classes. Memorizing the Krebs citric acid cycle did give me some heartburn, however. Genetics (charting generations of the characteristics of those blasted fruit flies, *Drosophila melanogaster*) was a class I scraped through.

In Wildlife Ecology, I learned about an idea called *pattern recognition*. This concept explained that some animals and birds had such specific spatial requirements, their habitats could be measured. If those criteria were matched in another location, one could predict with reasonable accuracy that species requiring habitat of that type would indeed be found there. When young animals and birds of the year dispersed, looking for their own territories, they would settle into areas that matched the patterns of the habitats where they were raised.

Pattern recognition is something, I believe, that has applied to me in my work around the country. I grew up on big water. I love seeing it. I love playing on it. I love fishing. The islands were important because they protected the inner waters from the rougher waters of the big, open lake. The presence of water has been a factor in every location to which my family and I moved.

From our first "permanent" job in Michigan (*Great Lake State*), we moved to Minnesota (*Land of Ten Thousand Lakes*) for five years. Home in Minnesota was Walker, a comfortably small town located on the shores of beautiful Leech Lake. Though not a beautiful name, I often described the 100,000-acre lake as "maybe not a Great Lake, but a pretty damned good one." It was so large there were places where one could stand on the shore and not see the tree line on the other side of the lake.

Southeast Alaska fit my pattern recognition requirements: islands and water. Fishing is productive in the protected waters in and among the islands of the Tongass National Forest. Whales and mountains were bonuses. Alaska is now home ... But it all started for me in Upper Michigan.

Michigan's Upper Peninsula was covered by continental glaciers several thousand feet thick for millions of years. Several advances from the northwest were followed by retreats of the ice sheets, the last one some fourteen thousand years ago. The glaciers of the Wisconsin period began a slow withdrawal, revealing the basins of Lakes Huron, Michigan, and Erie that it had scooped out as they had advanced. The basins of Lakes Superior and Ontario were formed by volcanic activity. As the glaciers receded, meltwaters filled all the depressions, forming the Great Lakes. The peninsulas of what would become the State of Michigan divided the basins from one another.

The Niagara Escarpment (over which Niagara Falls plunge) arcs northwestward from Niagara through the Bruce Peninsula of Lake Huron, runs east-west through Michigan's Upper Peninsula, and then southwest through Wisconsin's Door Peninsula. This escarpment comprises a relatively durable cap of dolomitic limestone over a softer and more erodible shale. The ridge is the remnant shoreline of an Ordovician-Silurian-age tropical sea that existed over 400 million years ago. The limestone was formed by the deposition of calcium carbonate of algal and shell fragments. In places, dolomite (magnesium carbonate) was formed where magnesium was in abundance. In the 1950s, US Steel established a sizeable open pit limestone quarry on the mainland at Port Dolomite at the eastern end of the Les Cheneaux.

I grew up on the gentle southern slope of the Niagara Escarpment near the towns of Cedarville and Hessel. Both communities are located on the shores of Lake Huron, the second-largest of the five Great Lakes. Our towns were not exposed to the open waters of the "Big Lake." They were protected by an island archipelago (thirty-two named islands), collectively labeled the *Les Cheneaux* (lay shun oh) Islands, left behind by the glaciers. The low-lying islands range in size from less than an acre to the seven-mile-long Marquette Island. The highest point on any of the islands was probably no more than seventy-five feet above lake level.

We were told that Les Cheneaux was French for "the channels," but that point has been argued for decades. Cheneaux, according to some, does not appear to be an actual French word. It was common for locals to use a bastardized version of Les Cheneaux by shortening it to "The Snows" when referring to the area. Locally we had the Snows Channel, the Snows Bar, Our Lady of the Snows Catholic Church, and the Snows Resort. We also received a fair amount of snow, so The Snows was an apt moniker. As school kids attending Les Cheneaux Community Schools, we did, however, find that the more formal designation worked perfectly in a chant: "Les Cheneaux, Les Cheneaux, the more you go, the less you know." Yes, we were charmingly clever, and we were all, as Garrison Keillor described the children of his fictional Lake Woebegone, "above average."

The tiny lakeshore communities of Cedarville and Hessel are unincorporated villages sheltered by the islands. The former was named after the white cedar tree, highly valued for its light, strong, and aromatic lumber, and the latter named after two Swedish founders. Three miles of state highway M-134 separate the two towns. Both shared a common garbage dump located midway between the two during my childhood. The dump was on a slight rise just north of a county gravel road that paralleled the state highway.

Our end of the Upper Peninsula, specifically our island archipelago, is a biome that falls between the temperate deciduous forests to the south and the boreal forest further north in Canada. Our islands were covered chiefly with spruce, balsam fir, white cedar, white and red (Norway) pine. On well-drained ridges both on the islands and on the mainland, sugar maple, beech, and ash were the dominant hardwoods.

The marshy lake shore margins of the bays were rimmed by red maple, elm, and the more extensive balsam poplars, close relatives of cottonwoods. We knew balsam poplar as "balm-of-Gilead," *bam* for short. In the spring, long, gummy buds developed on its branches, buds from which emerged leaves and flowers. When the leaves and flowers emerged, the sticky scales of the buds were cast loose. In the spring, people were careful not to park their cars under bam trees, as those sticky scales would mar the finish. The resulting sappy marks couldn't be washed off. Instead, they had to be buffed out with a power buffer. Springtime had a unique smell in the Les Cheneaux... The pungent odor of bam trees waking from a long, frigid winter.

Eventually, I became curious about the origin of "balm-of-Gilead." I was surprised to find a biblical reference. This was a term used for an aromatic ointment used to make perfume and incense derived from a small Asiatic and African tree of the myrrh family. Myrrh was one of the three gifts carried by the three biblical wise men to Bethlehem 2000 years ago (gold and frankincense were the others). While bam trees weren't the source for myrrh, its pungent sap reminded folks of the actual "balm-of-Gilead," thus the common, though incorrect, name.

Bam grew fast and attained large diameters at a young age. Unfortunately, they weren't of much use as lumber. However, Dad pointed out that boards sawed from them could be used as sheathing for houses as long as the boards could be kept out of the weather. Bam was short-lived when compared with cedars, pine, and spruce. Their bright green leaves contrasted with the darker green of the evergreens that dominated the islands. Growing along creeks, they were favored by beavers that gnawed them down, stripped them of bark for food, and chewed them into shorter lengths for dam-building.

I was told that before a rain the leaves of balm-of-Gilead and the other poplars (bigtooth and quaking aspens) curled up, exposing their silvery undersides. When you looked across the dark, wind-whipped waters, these trees would form a silvery band between dark water and the deep gray rain clouds approaching. I learned later in life that tree leaves don't curl up as storms approach. What happens is that the leaves are oriented predominantly to the prevailing wind, so their dark upper sides are positioned to catch as much sunlight as possible. Storms move through with a shift in the wind, blowing the leaves in a different direction, exposing their lighter undersides.

Summers seemed all too short when I was growing up. I don't recall them being too hot, though I do recall an exceptional two days in a row in the early 1960s when the thermometers soared to ninety degrees. That was *hot*. Swimming was popular with us kids. Unless someone drove us to Bay City Lake, a state forest campground north of Hessel on an inland lake, we had to sneak down to the shore past one of the summer cottages. The shoreline was all privately owned, with no public swimming areas. We tracked which of the summer places wasn't occupied, especially those places whose owners had eliminated the bulrushes, dumped sand on their beach, and installed a dock from which we could cannonball into the cool lake. Sometimes we misjudged our timing, and the owners or nosy neighbors would materialize and shoo us away.

Summers meant more tourists crowding the streets of both our towns. They caught our perch, our pike, our bass. I liked summer, but I didn't like tourists.

"I wish we didn't have to put up with tourists," I told Dad as a pre-teen.

Dad shrugged. "If it weren't for people coming up here in the summer, I wouldn't have a job," he said. "We couldn't afford to live here," he added. That caused me to reconsider.

Summers also meant fishing for yellow perch in the channels, and when the May flies hatched in early June, the lake herring entered the bays to feed. We would fish off the docks of absent summer people when we could get away with it, but all too often we were ordered off the dock by a neighbor or caretaker.

With fall came the dramatic change in the colors of the woods that draped our gentle topography. The soft and hard maples on dry hardwood ridges turned brilliant crimson and gold, respectively. In the dark green conifer forests that dominated the islands, patches of white birch and quaking aspen turned bright yellow, quite a contrast with the leaden gray skies typical of stormy autumns.

Mallards, black ducks, and teal migrated through the Snows, pausing in places like Duck Bay and Flower Bay to load up on the wild rice. Diving ducks like the bluebills and redheads preferred the open water but the soft mud lake bottoms beneath channels and bays provided feed in the form of insect larvae, mollusks, and wild celery. Brushy duck blinds were built on all the good points of land and refurbished annually. Popular blinds were occupied nearly every day of every duck season.

Fall would ease into winter in November most years. Down-staters flooded the Upper Peninsula for the deer season that always began on November 15 and ran through November 30. Many hunters would have driven five or more hours, coming from Lansing, Grand Rapids, or even Flint and Detroit.

Of course, I resented the influx of guys dressed in red and green plaid woolen mackinaws. They crowded the grocery stores and the bars and tromped into the Bon-Air in their Sorel™ boots to buy bottles of whiskey. They laughed and called each other names, often referring to their own prowess as a hunter or their companions' lack of skill.

When I told Mom that I wished they had to hunt in their

own counties, she explained that "a lot of those people work in factories all year long. They live for these two weeks they get to spend up here hunting." I lived in this unique place, a place that people worked hard for fifty weeks a year in factories Down Below just for the opportunity to visit for two weeks.

Most of us of deer hunting age hoped for at least a little snow by mid-November when deer season opened. "Tracking snow," we called it. We wished only for enough snow to tell where the deer had been and where they were going. Deer in their gray winter coats were easier for hunters to spot in the snow-covered woods than they were without snow. And, of course, blood trails left behind by any deer so unlucky as to be wounded would also be easier to follow when tracking.

During the many years I hunted out of a deer camp on one of the islands, we would often stand outside on our cabin porch listening to the wind and the waves. We were sheltered from the wind at the camp, but we could tell where we would be hunting that day by the sound of the wind-driven waves of the big lake crashing on the outside shore. If we could hear the dull roar of the surf, we would be hunting within walking distance of the camp. In the absence of that low, far-off rumble, we might take a boat ride around the outside of the island to conduct a deer drive on one of several points the deer favored.

Winters were accompanied by snow several feet deep. In rare years we would get cold snaps in late November or early December that would cause the channels to freeze over with clear ice several inches thick. Blue ice, it was called, though to me it appeared to be clear. We could skate for miles on that ice. Enterprising kids would build hand-held kites that would propel them to speeds bound to cause severe damage if they hit snow drifts. That pleasure was usually short-lived when the first of our annual average of 180 inches of snow began accumulating.

Winter was also a time for ice fishing. The more industrious of us had fish shanties, tar paper shacks constructed on a two-by-four platform and heated by small wood stoves. Before snowmobiles became common in the later 1960s, fish shanties were towed out on the ice by hand or by small four-wheel-drive "bugs." These vehicles often began their lives as Jeeps but in their old age were stripped of their bodies, with wooden benches installed in place of upholstered seats and all four tires adorned with chains.

This was where I began life. We spent some seasons in Spring Bay up the St. Mary's River from Detour Village in my years before entering grade school and one year in Oregon my freshman year in high school. Cedarville and Hessel, however, were always home to me. I grew up there. Looking back, it's where I learned a lot about life.

Names have been changed in many of the following stories to protect privacy.

Midnight Notes

I SHOT MY FATHER WHEN I WAS THREE.

I don't remember it, but according to eyewitnesses, I marched out of the bedroom with my gun, walked right up to my father, aimed at his chest, and pulled the trigger.

I don't know for sure if he ever got over it. It might have tainted our relationship for the next fifty years.

It wasn't my fault. My parents were the ones who had given me a cork gun for Christmas.

Our relationship didn't follow the traditional path of father and son. I was born to my seventeen-year-old mother during my dad's hitch in the Army during the Korean War. Dad was home for my birth but then gone for the next year and a half. I was walking and talking by the time of his discharge, when he showed up out of nowhere and moved in on my mother and me. She said that I clammed up, refusing to speak. Just who was this stranger who demanded my mother's attention—and, maddeningly for me, received it elaborately?

Dad wasn't one to show much emotion. He was always serious. He was always working. There was no idle time for him. Rarely did I hear him laugh. He was quick to anger and struggled to keep it in check. When he reached the boiling point, it sometimes resulted in a spanking if I were the focus of his attention.

He never praised me but was quick to criticize. As he saw it, praise just made people think they were better than others.

We were different people, for sure. Dad had quit school in the tenth grade. If my grandmother had given her permission, he would have joined the Army in 1945, joining his older brothers in the war. The wars in Europe and the Pacific both ended before Dad could join the Army. He quit school anyway and went to work.

I never saw my dad with a book, rarely saw him reading a newspaper. On the other hand, I was reading before the other kids in school. "I don't know how you can sit there with a book all day," Dad once said to me as I lay on the couch one rainy day, my nose in an Isaac Asimov novel.

School, at least the academic aspect, was too easy for me. Straight As were the rule rather than the exception. One day in my senior year of high school, I came home with three academic awards for excellence. Coming home aglow, I saw Dad in the garage. I announced that I'd received three awards that day.

"Well, that's three more than I ever got," he said, glancing up from his project on the workbench. I was crestfallen. I'd hoped that he would offer congratulations or a "good for you"— some indication that he was proud of me. I sure didn't get that impression.

I moved away, got married, and had kids of my own. The decades passed, and I grew to understand Dad more because, in many ways, we were similar. Sometimes we didn't say the right things, not because of spite, but because we were both somewhat awkward socially, and when taken by surprise, often the first words out of our mouths were not the words we'd have chosen if we'd had time to think about them.

Our relationship improved. After Dad passed away, my sister and I hosted a gathering in his memory. Relatives and friends came to express their condolences and share their stories about Dad. Many of the stories I'd never heard.

One of Dad's best friends, his cousin Jack Tassier, recalled the story Dad had told him about the night that I'd left Dad a note on the kitchen table about owing him a new bumper. Jack said that Dad had been pretty unhappy about the bumper but, after thinking about it, thought it pretty funny that I'd left him a note in the middle of the night.

What had happened was that late one night, I came home from an evening of hockey followed by beer at the Cedarville Bar. The car slid off the road on an icy corner, stranding it up on a snowbank at the edge of the road. I tried to back the car off the snowbank with no success. As I was only fifty feet from our driveway, I left the car running and walked to the garage, and fired up the old weapons carrier (Dodge M-37), a Korean War-era army surplus four-wheel-drive truck....You know the kind, with the wooden racks on the back and fold-down wooden benches where the troops sat while being transported.
The truck also had a winch on the front bumper. I pulled up to the back of the car, ran out the cable and hooked it onto the bumper. I wasn't about to crawl under the car to hook the cable around the axle. I slowly backed the weapons carrier away from the car and tightened the cable. The car wouldn't pull off the snowbank, so I gave it a little jerk. The car still wouldn't come. I gave it a bigger jerk. No luck.

I got out to check what might be wrong. Well, I'd forgotten to take the car out of park. Worse, I'd bent the rear bumper of the car, pulling one side off at an angle. I put the car in neutral and it slid out just fine. I parked the car and the weapons carrier back in the garage. Sick about the bumper, I thought I'd better not surprise my dad in the morning, so I left a note on the kitchen table: "Dad. I owe you a new bumper. Pete"

Late the next morning, I got up and faced the music. I'd figured I'd be taking the car to a repair shop and pay a professional to fix the bumper, but Dad had figured out what needed to be done. His idea wasn't me getting off easy by taking the car to a shop. With a queasy stomach and a headache, I unbolted the bumper and straightened it out with a sledgehammer. Hammering on the bumper on the concrete floor seemed to echo in my aching head. Dad was there the whole time, seeming to enjoy my extreme discomfort. After a couple of hours, I finished the project and the bolted bumper back onto the car. Not much was said, not that much needed to be said.

"Yeah," Jack said, "that note really saved your bacon. He was proud of you for working on that bumper while you were hung over and never complaining about it."

When Jack finished, I realized that Dad and I were alike in some ways. Neither of us was comfortable with emotions. Dad left notes for me when I wasn't there, notes that I'd find when he wasn't there, not written notes but stories that showed he'd taken pride in some of the things that I had done for something that he valued.

Thirty years ago, a friend told me a story that Dad had related to him one day.

I'd been working a summer job mowing grass for

minimum wage at an association of summer homes owned by wealthy people. There were many common areas, lawns, and fields. It was a constant effort to keep the grass cut. We would start at one end, and by the time we reached the other, it was time to start again at the beginning with our push mowers.

It was hot, sweaty work. Most of the kids hired to do the job would quit and head for the workshop when it began to rain. It wasn't pleasant mowing in the rain. It was almost noon one day when, as Jim Haske and I were cutting one of the fields, it began raining. Jim and I conferred and decided we could get that field cut despite the rain before heading to the shop to eat our lunches.

We pushed our mowers back and forth in the steady rain, finishing the job while the grass was dry enough to mow before shutting down and heading back to the shop late for lunch. The owner of one of the summer homes walked past us on the sidewalk. He stopped by the shop where the rest of the crew, including Dad, was at lunch.

He announced to the group that he'd seen two kids out cutting grass in the rain and during their lunch. "It's been a long time since that's happened," he marveled. Dad, by passing that on to his friends, had left me that note to find eventually.

Another time while I was still in college, an older friend of the family congratulated me. He said that Dad had told him that one of the people I worked for in the summer had offered to back me with an interest-free loan if I continued to graduate school. That was information I'd shared with only my parents, but Dad had passed that along with a bit of pride. It was another note Dad had left for me.

I wish I had recognized that we couldn't relive the past while he was still here. Today I can say, *Dad, thank you for the notes you left behind for me to find the next morning.*

Birthplace

My birthplace just south of Cedarville on the southeast corner of the Four Mile Block was an old, framed cabin sided with vertical half-log siding painted white. Originally it had been one room, but my parents had added a divider to the left of the entryway to afford some privacy for their bedroom. The linoleum was curled up near the walls and made tacky noises when walked upon.

I was born in that cabin. Dad was home on leave, presumably for the birth of his first child. When the time came that evening, Dad ran the seventy-five feet to his sister Rhoda's house next door to call Doc Blue. The story I heard was that when Doc Blue arrived at the cabin, he demanded $20 payment *up front* from Dad. When Dad said he didn't have $20, Doc Blue said he wouldn't be attending the birth without cash in hand. In the middle of the night, Dad left Mom and Doc Blue to get his former construction crew boss (and cousin), Al Pollard, out of bed for a loan. By the time Dad had returned, I'd been born. I always wondered if Doc Blue had demanded immediate payment to get Dad out of the cabin and out of his way while Doc was handling the birth.

After I was born, they added a door at the end of their

bedroom and tacked on a ten-foot by twelve-foot addition where they placed my crib. For heat, a Duo-Therm fuel oil space heater stood in the middle of the cabin. Our outhouse was tucked into the edge of the woods about fifty feet from the front door. I remember my Dad one day proudly showing off his modification to the outhouse. Alongside the adult-sized seat, he had cut down the bench and added a lower seat just the right size for a kid just graduating from diapers.

The balsam fir, birch, and spruce woods beyond the outhouse was a great place to play. Just a hundred feet to the east, a pond at the end of a gravel pit was a haven for frogs. Our yard, a gap in the trees between our cabin and my aunt's house to the east, had patches of grass and clover. One day I found a large yellow and black insect buzzing among the clover blossoms. It couldn't fly, so I picked it up, thinking I could help it. It resulted in my first-ever bumble bee sting. It was also my first experience in trying to help when help had not been requested.

That cabin was also where I took my first steps on the way to becoming a skeptic. At the first Christmas, I remember, we had a small Christmas tree located about as far from the space heater as possible. I'd heard all the stories about Santa visiting the homes of all the good little boys and girls. Allegedly, he slid down chimneys to deliver gifts. I didn't think Santa Claus was going to fit in the little six-inch stove pipe that came out the back of the space heater.

On Christmas morning, there were gifts under the tree. I was excited about that. Then I went to the front door and turned the doorknob. I had to pull it open with a jerk as the door tended to stick shut during cold weather. Two inches of fresh snow from the day before had settled on the older mantle of dirty snow. Looking out on the glaring white scene, I observed our quiet neighborhood. To close the door, I had to bump it shut with my shoulder.

"What were you looking at?" Mom asked.

"I know Santa Claus didn't come down our stove pipe. He must have used the door. But I didn't see any tracks." I was well on the road to skepticism.

It was this place where we got our first pet, a small male pup from Aunt Margaret and Uncle Harvey, who lived up the street. Their daughters Jo (now Jodi) and Susie had a small female named Mimi that gave birth to a litter of pups. Mom and Dad eventually named this nondescript grayish pup with a light brown saddle. They liked to see an animal develop its own personality before giving it a name. I never realized how much of a sense of humor my parents had until years later. I have yet to encounter anyone who, as a child, had a pet called "Nameless."

We were moving up in the world. Dad was working forty-eight hours a week at the Les Cheneaux Club, an association of wealthy summer homeowners on the Club Point of Marquette Island. He painted boat houses, repaired leaking faucets, put up cabinetry, rid attics of bats, and about whatever else needed doing in those huge old houses that the wealthy owners called their "cottages."

Jerry's Place

I WAS JUST OUT OF KINDERGARTEN IN 1958 when Mom and Dad bought cousin Jerry Griffin's house on the corner. It was just a couple hundred yards east of us, down the road that was the southern side of the Four Mile Block. My sister and I still refer to it as "Jerry's Place" sixty years later.

We entered our new house through the back door accessed by three steps up to a small, uncovered porch with no railing. Inside the back door, a small landing led to a set of creaky wooden stairs to the basement.

The basement was dark and damp, housing a coal-fired furnace and a green hopper that was my job to keep filled with coal shoveled from a small bin. In one corner of the basement, there was a speed bag, a little inflated leather bag suspended from a wooden plate attached to a floor joist. Dad bought two pairs of boxing gloves to teach me how to box. He could make that speed bag bounce upward off its supporting plate with a blow from his right hand, and by the time it bounced back downward, he hit it again with his left, causing a steady, rhythmic beat. I was never able to achieve that steady rhythm, perhaps an early indication that his boxing lessons would never take with me.

Alternatively, by a ninety-degree turn to the left from the back door to the house, you entered the eat-in kitchen. One nine-pane window faced south, while another nine-pane window over the sink overlooked the garage and most of our L-shaped driveway with one entrance on the east-west Four Mile Block Road and the other on the north-south road now known as Tassier Avenue.

Beyond the kitchen and through an archway was our living room with two picture windows: one looking out on the driveway and the other facing north toward the Four Mile Block Road. This living room had a red brick fireplace! Our little black and white television with the rabbit-ears rested on a stand next to the fireplace. My parents were disappointed when they came one day to find that my little sister Terrie and I had run our crayons along every gray mortar joint between bricks on the fireplace. The wax couldn't be scrubbed off with soap and water. Under parental supervision, Terrie and I tried. Those crayon marks remained as long as we lived there.

While that home had only two bedrooms, it had a bathroom and tub indoors. My sister and I had shared a two-tier bunk bed for our first year or so. Eventually, Dad raised the roof on one side of the house. Rudy Pierson, a local contractor and deer-hunting friend of Dad's, used a crane to lift the roof while Dad inserted a prefabricated two-by-four stud wall under the edge of the roof. The resulting space was converted into two second-floor bedrooms, one each for Terrie and me.

We took in a boarder one winter for a couple of months that year. Whether it was abusive situations at home (that were never talked about) or failing marriages complicated by high school-aged children at home (not spoken of in front of the children), it was not uncommon for families to take in relatives' children. Ours was a high school senior, the elder son of a marriage that failed years ago.

He and I shared my upstairs bedroom, each with our single bed on opposite sides of the room. Our boarder was a funny guy, and I liked being around him.

Neither of my parents admonished him for smoking a pipe. Maybe they doubted their influence over him at that stage of life. Mom packed his school lunch every day. Terrie and I were on the hot lunch program. Mom made him sandwiches spread with potted meat, the only kind of sandwich he would eat. I remember wrinkling up my nose in disgust at the smell of potted meat from a freshly opened can. And here I was, a guy who loved SPAM™.

Late one quiet night in our shared bedroom, I heard our boarder get up. The floor creaked as he made his way across the room. The springs sagged as he sat on the edge of my bed briefly before crawling under the covers with me.

"You can't tell anybody what we did," he said when he was done. It wasn't a threat. It was more of a plea.

Some nights he was in my bed. Some nights I was in his. It always ended the same way: "Don't tell anybody."

Finally, he graduated. He moved far away, and I rarely ever crossed paths with him. He died several years ago after a prolonged illness.

I was a good kid. I never told anybody.

Our "new" house also had a basement with a coal-fired boiler that fed hot water to the heavy cast iron radiators located in every room. My jobs were to shovel coal from the coal bin into the green hopper that fed coal to the furnace and to clean out the "clinkers," the rock-like nuggets produced by burning coal. I dumped the clinkers in a designated low spot a hundred feet from the house.

We had a big yard and a two-car garage heated by a wood stove. Jerry had repaired cars in that heated garage. Dad's imagination was unleashed when he thought of having his own place to work on cars and other projects out of the weather.

Dad and my uncles loved tinkering with their "bugs," four-wheel-drive vehicles with their bodies removed, exposing the chassis and engine. Each fenderless tire was draped in chains for traction in the snow. A straight wooden bench replaced the standard upholstered front seat that had come with the vehicle. Some had windshields still attached, others did not. "Bugs" were used for churning through the snowy woods or to and from fish shanties on Muskellunge Bay. Tinkering with or constructing "bugs" in a garage heated with a wood stove was a family sport and often the center of fraternal gatherings. Dad and uncles gathered around such vehicles in the evening, a can of Stroh's beer in one hand and an unfiltered Camel cigarette in the other.

As a pre-teen, I loved hanging around garages that smelled of wood smoke, cigarettes, grease, and oil, while the old guys told stories [Author's note: "old" guys! Dad was barely thirty years old at the time!]. One night, Dad, his brothers Wenton and Kenny, and cousin Ernie Griffin were in our garage at our just-acquired home on the corner, drinking beer and smoking. Ernie's bug was parked over the five-foot deep hole in one of the garage stalls, a pit that allowed a guy to stand up while changing oil or greasing the underside of a vehicle. I left them and went to the house.

I asked Mom if I could have a beer to take to the garage, too. That wasn't happening. But Mom, displaying a sense of humor that I did not come to appreciate for many years, rinsed out an empty Stroh's beer can. Then she carefully filled it with milk through the larger of the two little triangular can opener holes that had been punched in the top. I went back to the garage.

"What the hell," Uncle Wenton exclaimed when he caught sight of me sipping from the can just like the adults. He took the can from me and tipped it until he saw the milk spill. The adults laughed as he handed me my "beer" back. I figured it would be too much to ask for an unfiltered Camel.

Sometimes it takes years to connect events from the past. Four days before Christmas in 1961, Ernie and Uncle Wenton plunged through the ice while riding that bug on the way to their fish shanty on Musky Bay. Uncle Wenton, though unable to swim, made it to the edge of the ice and hung on until rescuers pulled him out. Ernie, however, did not. I will never forget the look on Dad's face when relatives came to the door and told him that Ernie was dead, and they were undertaking a body recovery effort. It took several hours to recover his body. It was the first time that anyone I knew had died.

"Never trust the ice," I tell people to this day. It's never safe. In the decades since Ernie's passing, other family members have died as a result of misjudging the safety of the ice.

Dad was working at the Club. He had a good relationship with Dick Smith, the Les Cheneaux Club caretaker who lived on Marquette Island, as well as the rest of the crew. It wasn't long, however, before I began hearing Dad expressing his opinion of various club members to Mom. A few of them, he said, were considerate people who treated the workers kindly. Others, well, Dad just shook his head. He was always bringing home stories about monied people and how dissociated they were from the real world.

He once told Mom of a conversation he had with one of the Club members. He had just finished replacing a sink in the kitchen of one of the cottages. The owner, feeling generous, told Dad he could have the old sink if he wanted.

"If you have running water," he added apologetically, perhaps thinking he had insulted Dad in assuming he lived in a house with running water.

"Yes, I have running water," Dad said coldly, "and I have hot water heat, too." We were only a year or so removed from a space heater, an outhouse, and a pitcher pump on the sink, and Dad might have been a bit sensitive.

Dad didn't much care for club members who looked down on the men who worked there. He told us about helping another crew member carry a sofa from the road that encircled the point up from the lakeside homes. Carrying the cumbersome piece of furniture from the road to the house, they had difficulty staying to the sidewalk. When the workmen encountered a number of the cottage owner's family who refused to yield the sidewalk, Dad and his helper were forced to step off the sidewalk with their load to allow the family members to pass.

That attitude wasn't limited to the human members of the families, either. Dad described having a job replacing a light fixture in a bedroom. When he walked into the bedroom, the family schnauzer was napping on the bed. The dog took a look at Dad, stood up, turned its back on him, and laid down again, facing the opposite direction.

I didn't know it then, but the Les Cheneaux Club would come to play an important role in my life for several years.

Gravy Boat

BY 1960, WE HAD FAR MORE COMPANY AT JERRY'S PLACE than we had ever had in our little log cabin. One late summer day not long after we moved in, Dad's cousin Steve Tassier was over. Dad and Steve drank a couple of cans of Stroh's that afternoon while Mom prepared a pork roast for dinner.

Roast pork was one of my favorite meals. The house was filled with an enticing smell. After boiling the potatoes, Mom made gravy. "Supper's just about ready," she said to Dad and Steve.

Steve rose to leave, and Dad followed him to the back door. They stepped out on the porch … and stepped right back inside.

"There's a deer in the yard," Dad whispered. Mom, Terrie, and I hurried to the back door and stuck our heads out to take a look at the little doe. It was feeding the rich, green grass just down the hill from our septic tank.

Dad and Steve grinned at each other and whispered. Mom knew what was going on. "No, Pete," she insisted, shaking her head.

Dad disappeared into the bedroom and emerged carrying

his Winchester .308. He snapped the magazine in place, pulled back the bolt, and eased a shell into the chamber. Terrie and I were watching out the bathroom window that overlooked the backyard.

"You kids get away from the windows," he said, "You don't want you to watch this." Then he and Steve were out the back door on the porch.

"No, no, no!" Mom insisted, again, but in vain. I knew she didn't have anything against hunting because she used to hunt deer with Dad. She had her own Winchester .308.

"POW!"

I'd never been that close to a rifle discharge. The explosion filled our house.

Dad came back in with the rifle.

"Goddammit, Pete!" my mother shouted at my father. Tight-lipped, she looked at the kitchen table set for dinner: the pork roast, the boiled potatoes, the little dish of canned tomatoes at each setting, and the ceramic cream-colored gravy boat filled with steaming gravy.

She snatched up the gravy boat and, without hesitation, hurled it, not at Dad, but directly through the center pane of our south-facing kitchen window. "Why?" she yelled.

Terrie and I looked at the hole in the window, looked at each other, and scattered, each of us scurrying to a place where we felt sheltered from the stand-off in the kitchen. It was the first time I'd ever witnessed angry words between my parents. To a seven-year-old and a five-year-old, it was like the end of the world.

Years later, Terrie and I had a week alone with Dad after his terminal diagnosis. Dad's wife had graciously let us have that week with Dad to ourselves by leaving to visit her out-of-state daughters.

I reminded Dad of that day nearly five decades in the past.

"I'd never seen Mom get as mad as that day she threw the gravy boat through the kitchen window at Jerry's place when you shot that deer."

Dad looked surprised.

"I didn't shoot it," he said defensively. "Steve killed that deer."

I am glad he cleared that up. Both Dad and Steve are gone now. At a recent beach party, I regaled Steve's son Mike with the story about Mom heaving the gravy boat through the window when his dad shot a deer out of season from our back porch.

Lady

ONE DAY IN THE SPRING OF 1962, Dad brought home two raccoon kits from the Club. Their faces had the characteristic raccoon mask, a band of dark fur across its face like the Long Ranger's mask in contrast to the light gray fine fur covering the rest of their bodies. Their tails had dark rings on them, just like raccoons in the magazines. Before their eyes opened, we fed them warm milk from a toy baby bottle that Terrie used for one of her dolls.

Their mother had the audacity to nest in one of the boat houses leaving raccoon droppings all over the nicely varnished mahogany Chris-Craft boats. She had her family nest between the ceiling on the first floor of the boathouse and the second story floor. Dad said the crew had lit sulfur candles in an effort to drive her out, but she had stayed in place, spreading her body out between the floor joists to block the acrid sulfur smells from getting to her newborns. Dad had apparently been touched by the sacrifice this mother raccoon made to protect her young and brought home the two surviving kits of the litter, one female and one male.

The little male 'coon died not long after Dad brought them home. When our surviving raccoon was weaned from her bottle, we started feeding her Purina Puppy Chow™ and food scraps. As she grew, she began to "wash" her kibble and food scraps in her water dish before eating. We thought it was cute. When we looked it up in our new *Encyclopedia Americana* set, we learned that soaking the food in water made it easier for her because raccoons lacked salivary glands. Wetting the food made it easier to swallow and digest. *[Author's note: This is not true, as we now know! Wetting its paws increases tactile sensations that allow a raccoon to determine what it is about to eat and how best to get it into its mouth.]*

When she was several weeks old, Mom took her to the vet in Pickford. She hoped to get our raccoon vaccinated for rabies. Doc Barber said that wasn't possible as vaccinating raccoons for rabies usually gave them rabies. It wasn't the last time our raccoon went to see the vet.

Lady, as we named her, liked to climb on the backs of our over-stuffed living room chairs. She would run her paws down the back of visitors' necks, under their collars, and through their hair—behavior that we later learned to be typical of raccoons. Lady explored unseen places with her delicate and sensitive paws in search of food. Many of our guests gasped in surprise and said it gave them goose bumps.

Her explorations were often accompanied by soft trills sounding a bit like a cat's purr, but higher pitched. She also had a curious short, high-pitched, three-note call, a nasal *weee-ooo-eee*. It was a call she used when looking for us, which I took to mean "I'm lonely and want company."

Lady was a curious and playful animal. One day my

mother heard a clicking noise coming from the master bedroom. When she investigated, she found Lady sprawled out on her back on top of the pillows at the head of the bed. She was pulling the dangling chain of the reading light clamped onto the headboard. She was turning the light on and off, fascinated with her newfound power to defeat the dark.

That raccoon was pretty doggoned smart, too. She located the bread drawer in our lower cabinets when we were out one day. She pulled the drawer open and feasted on the bread and donuts found within. Mom knew how to make the bread drawer raccoon-proof. She inserted a wooden yardstick down through the pull handles on the vertical drawers. Lady would have to remove the yardstick to open the bread drawer. Problem solved.

Until one day when we came home from school. Lady had pulled the yardstick up far enough to clear the handle of the bread drawer before pulling it open and helping herself to the contents once again. Subsequently, we bought a metal bread box with a latch even a clever raccoon with incredibly manipulative paws could not open.

Lady disappeared from our yard one evening. We did not see again for a week. Then at dusk one day, we heard her *weee-ooo-eee* call from the dark woods. We responded with our poor imitation of her "I'm lonely" call, and she came limping into the open yard. We saw that she'd been shot in the back with fine shot, probably at a distance. Mom took her to the vet, who applied gentian violet to the wounds, and she eventually recovered. I was beginning to see a disadvantage to wild animals raised by humans because they developed no natural fear of people.

Later that fall, she disappeared again, and we had no idea

where she was. We feared the worst. But then my mother found Lady curled up in a nest under the house. She was hibernating, we thought. We kept an eye on her over the winter. She was groggy, not entirely awake, not entirely asleep. And when spring arrived, her activity increased, and she resumed her normal inquisitive personality. The house was filled again with her trills. That summer, she was nearly fully grown at twenty pounds. She became increasingly distant, leaving us for longer and longer periods. And then she didn't return. We thought, or maybe *hoped*, that perhaps she had figured out that she was a raccoon, that it was time to live in the woods and find a mate. We never saw her again.

In 1963, Sterling North published his book "Rascal." It was a true story about a boy growing up during World War I and his adventures with his pet raccoon, Rascal. I read and re-read that book, smiling at his observations about raccoons, observations that fit my experiences with our pet raccoon, Lady.

At one of our monthly Boy Scout gatherings, we were participants in an 'evening coon hunt.' We met up with several local men who had 'coon hounds.

They set the hounds loose in an area likely to harbor raccoons. When the hounds began baying, the hounds' owners and a pack of boys armed with flashlights began pursuing them into the dark cedar and spruce woods. Eventually, the hounds treed the raccoon and the group of boys and men caught up with them. I'm not sure how, in recalling that night, they got that raccoon out of the tree. But they did. When it hit the ground, the hounds were on it. Everybody stood in a loose circle and watched the fight in its entirety, except for me. I hung at the

back of the crowd. I didn't much care for the spectacle.
    Still don't.

Rafting Flower Bay

IN THE EARLY 1960s, Dad had taken a seasonal maintenance job with the federal government at Kincheloe Air Force Base in Kinross, some twenty miles north of Cedarville. Kincheloe was part of a network of Strategic Air Command bases that hosted a fleet of B-52 bombers and tankers for mid-air re-fueling. It was steady work and paid well.

I remember he and Mom struggling with the government job application, an SF-171, a form I later came to know well. Dad recalled every job he'd ever had, what he did for that job, when he was employed, and what his pay was. Mom would write it down on the form. That was her job, filling out the paperwork. She did our taxes, balanced our checkbook, and applied for all our antlerless deer hunting permits.

Mom took a job as a teller at the local branch of the First National Bank of St. Ignace. I remember her saying that she had inquired why the other teller was paid more than she was for doing the same work. The answer, unsatisfactory then, even more so now, was that "he had a family to support." That ended that discussion.

In the summer of 1963, I was eleven and my sister, Terrie,

nine. With Mom and Dad both working, they weren't about
to let us spend days on our own. They arranged for our grandmother, Ione Steel, to watch us at her newly constructed house
on Flower Bay. She and my grandfather had been recently
divorced. With her settlement, she had built a one-story home
with red cedar siding and an attached garage. It featured a
vaulted ceiling in her living room with large picture windows
facing Flower Bay and a greenstone fireplace. A painting by
Oliver Birge that had hung above the mantle of her and Grandpa's fireplace in Spring Bay now hung over her fireplace.

That painting was a story in a picture: a hunter lay
sprawled in the snow, his snowshoes tangled, the hunter's dog
taking chase after a deer, pulling the sled with the hunter's
rifle still in the scabbard attached to the sled. Grandma's hand-
carved wooden loom upon which she wove rag rugs stood on the
backside of her living room. Nearby was her easel, often with a
partially finished oil landscape painting on it.

I don't know about Terrie, but I found it a delight to
traipse around the cedar and balsam woods surrounding her
home. I chased frogs on the marshy shoreline and found oddly-
shaped and colored mushrooms in the woods. There were ducks
and herons and redwing blackbirds in the marsh.

One day Grandma gestured toward a point of land on Hill
Island on the other side of Flower Bay. The Shady Side Resort
on that point was owned and operated by her and Grandpa for
several years. They rented cabins and small boats to their guests.
One evening she took a client out fishing to show him where
and how to fish. She cast her bait into the dark waters of the
channel between Hill Island and the mainland and caught six
species of fish on her first six casts.

I tried fishing for trout in Flower Creek. Mom had told me that the state had planted trout in the creek when she and my uncle were just kids living at Shady Side. It hadn't taken long for the two of them to fish the creek out, she said. Tony's Trout Ponds were located just upstream on the north side of M-134, and I kept hoping that perhaps some of the fish he stocked in his ponds would escape into the creek.... But that was in vain.

I tried fishing from shore at Grandma's house, but I couldn't cast my bait beyond the weeds. When the wild rice began to emerge in Flower Bay, I wished I had a boat to get out further from the shore and into the rice-free channel only fifty feet from the muddy shore. Unfortunately, Grandma didn't have a boat.

Undeterred, I decided to build a raft that I could pole out to the good fishing spots in deeper water. Grandma's lot had been cleared to build her house. During construction, trees and stumps were pushed into piles at the edge of her lot. Some of the small white cedar and balsam fir had been cut into short lengths easily handled by the guys clearing the lot. Those smaller diameter logs were between six and eight feet long.

I spent half a day pulling out a dozen logs, poles really, small enough for an eleven-year-old to handle. One by one, I dragged them to the water's edge. My Boy Scout Manual showed the kind of knots I could use to bundle logs together for a raft, but I didn't have enough rope. So, I improvised.

Around the foundation of Grandma's new house, I'd found a lot of discarded 16-penny nails, some straight, some bent. I gathered them into a Hills Brothers Coffee™ can, the one with the red label and an old guy in a yellow nightshirt drinking coffee. I borrowed a hammer from Grandma and spent an hour straightening the bent nails.

I laid out the logs for my raft side-by-side at the shore. Then I laid scraps of two-by-fours across the logs at right angles. I hammered my nails through the two-by-fours into the logs. The result was a raft that barely floated but seemed to hold together.

Grandma wasn't really excited at the thought of me on a raft which might be swept away by the barely discernible current through the deepest channel of Flower Bay. She unwrapped a new pack of clothesline purchased at Hudson's hardware, tied one end to the raft and the other to a stake she had driven into the mud at the water's edge. She didn't want me drifting away in the current. Life jackets were optional as far as she was concerned.... Not that we had life jackets at the time.

On my first voyage, I poled the raft unsteadily through the wild rice. In a gap in the emerging rice, I saw a sun-dappled bottom about three feet down, and there, slowly finning its way along the bottom, was the biggest largemouth bass I'd ever seen. It saw me at the same time, and—in a swirl of mud—it suddenly disappeared.

"Grandma, I just saw the biggest fish I've ever seen," I yelled. I poled the raft back to shore, threw my fishing pole and some mayflies in a jar for bait on the raft, and poled back out. I never caught that bass, but the perch ... *Oh, the perch.* The yellow perch were biting!

Terrie joined me on the raft for perch fishing. Our combined weight caused the raft to sink just below the water surface. I nailed on some additional plywood scraps for extra flotation. We had so little freeboard that if a perch flopped off our hooks and landed on the raft, that fish usually swam to freedom through the gaps between the logs before we could corral it with our hands and add it to our stringer.

Nearby fishermen in their tin boats often laughed as they watched us try to capture fish swimming to freedom from our raft.

Grandma snapped a photograph of us standing on the raft. She reproduced the scene of Terrie and me fishing from the raft that summer in a watercolor painting. That watercolor hangs in my home. It was our first experience with a raft, but not our last.

A Home on the Water

In 1964, with both Mom and Dad employed, they felt empowered to purchase a summer home from Mrs. Supplee, an aging summer resident of the Snows. The home was located near the eastern end of the Les Cheneaux on Joker Bay, accessed by Lakeside Road from M-134. We now owned one hundred feet of lake shore at the exorbitant price of thirty-five dollars per foot of shoreline.

The house had been more of a summer home than a full-time residence. The entrance was accessed by a flight of wooden steps that led to a small landing at the kitchen door. The interior walls were covered in Celotex™ light brown wall-board. The upstairs included two bedrooms that my sister and I occupied, along with a kitchen, small dining area, and living room. An upstairs screened-in porch on the lake side of the house supported by six-by-six timbers was a delightful feature. We could be "outside" without being plagued by mosquitoes. Mom and Dad slept below in the walk-out basement.

Dad installed a monkey dock. With a heavy wooden maul, he had driven a pair of cedar poles every six feet out into the lake until he reached a depth that would float a boat. He nailed cedar 2x4 cross pieces between each pair of stakes and then laid eight-foot long 2x6 cedar planks from one pair of stakes to the next. At the end of the monkey dock, he drove more cedar posts upon which to build a tin roof shelter for our newly revarnished Chris-Craft runabout.

In the shade of the shelter, a school of rock bass gathered beneath the Chris Craft. They were easy to catch, lured from under the boat with a worm threaded onto a hook. The school was dominated by one fish, much larger than the others. It would dart out from the shade to snap up the offered bait. Terrie and I caught that rock bass several times over the course of the summer. We always threw it back. Dad disparaged rock bass as too boney to eat and he claimed they stunk up the house when fried.

Dad invited one of his work acquaintances at the Air Force Base to move onto the lot with us. Roy and Velma, with two young children, moved their mobile home next to us. We had never lived on the water before, and it was great.

Several months after we'd gotten settled in, Mom and Dad invited a number of friends over for a big beach party complete with bonfire, food, beer, and music. Dad had assembled a Heathkit amplifier from a kit that had been a Christmas gift. He plugged the record player into the amplifier and pumped Johnny Cash, Hank Snow, and Marty Robbins out through a couple of big speakers.

My Grandmother on my Dad's side, Rose Borton, was there. The plan was for my sister and me to go home with Grandma Borton just before dark, so the adults could party on without having to worry about the kids.

The fire was burning, hot dogs were roasted, and the kids

fetched beers from the refrigerator for the adults. It was a beautiful evening. Everyone was outside between the walk-out-basement and the shore.

Over the noise of the party, I heard my mother call from the house. "Pete!" Then with increasing urgency. "PETE!"

Not understanding whether she was calling Dad or me, I ran up the stairs and into the house. Mom was attending to Grandma, who was sitting motionless, upright in a kitchen chair, a vacant stare, no expression on her face. "Get your dad! Call the doctor!" Mom said.

I ran back outside and down the stairs... "Dad! Dad! It's Grandma!" Dad took one look at me and knew something serious was going on. He bolted inside, got on the phone, and called up Doc DeLoof at his home. Doc showed up a few minutes later, his old blocky station wagon careening into the driveway with his grill-mounted emergency flashers alternating red and blue. He dragged his black doctor's bag out of the car and hurried up the stairs to see what he could do.

My sister and I were terrified. We were only ten and twelve, and had never been exposed to anybody who was deathly ill before.

Before long, the Doctor exited, followed by Mom and Dad. Grandma was OK, it seemed. She hadn't had a stroke but what the doctor called a "high blood pressure attack." Doc had given her some medication to get her blood pressure back down, and she was going to be OK. That was a relief. But the plan for my sister and me to spend the night at Grandma's was at risk.

The party continued until late that night. Eventually, the last of the laggards left, the lights were turned out, and Mom and Dad went to bed. They didn't think to turn off the record player or the amplifier.

An odd thing I have learned about fire is that most people who die in house fires don't die from flames. They die of smoke inhalation rather than burns. As a fire begins to heat up, smoke and uncombusted gases are released and fill the rooms. They rise to the ceiling, and as they build, the toxic gas levels slowly inch downward, sinking past the levels of sleepers. The victims often never wake up.

Late that night after the party, my mother did wake up ... To find the basement full of smoke. She shook Dad awake, and they realized the house was on fire. They had time to throw their guns out on the front lawn along with a couple of dresser drawers, but by then, the upstairs was ablaze.

They ran over to Roy and Velma's and called the fire department, and then ran back to the house to see what else they could do. Roy pulled on his clothes and ran out to help. He had fenced in the yard to keep their kids from wandering away and just the previous day had changed the position of the gate so as not to wear down a path across the lawn. He ran over the spot where the gate had been the day before and did a somersault across the fence.

Friends on Hill Island on the other side of the bay who had been at the party saw the flames, jumped in their car, and hurried back. Word had spread through the community as volunteer fire department members were called.

The fire department arrived and laid hoses. Someone thought to call my other Grandmother, Ione Steel. When she arrived, she ran into the midst of the scene. "Where are my kids? Where are my kids?" she cried. In the dark, she tripped over a fire hose, hit the ground hard, and was knocked unconscious.

When the fire burst through the attic and out the vents on the gable ends of the house, my parents figured they'd lost everything. By then, more friends and firefighters had shown up. Eventually, they brought the blaze under control. But the house was beyond salvage.

My sister and me? We both learned the news when my aunt and uncle came to Grandma Borton's in the pre-dawn hours to deliver the sad news. Despite Grandma's bout with high blood pressure, Mom and Dad had decided to let us go with Grandma to stay with her. They had debated the decision but agreed that they didn't want Grandma thinking that they didn't trust her with her grandchildren.

The next morning, Mom, Dad, Terrie, and I visited the scene. My aunt and uncle had advised us kids not to go inside to look. But we couldn't stay away.

The walls of the house were intact, but you could see where the fire had burned through the roof. Windows were broken out where the firemen had directed streams from their water hoses.

Inside, you could hardly draw a breath before choking. The smell of smoke was so thick you could taste it. It wasn't like a wood smoke smell. It was a terrible smell of burnt plastic, paint, and glue.

The upstairs walls were charred to the floor. The fire had started in the corner where the amplifier and record player were stacked. The floor there was deeply burned, and the wall burned through the studs and into the exterior siding. A beautiful wood mosaic coffee table that Mom and Dad's friend, Sam, had built while serving a prison sentence, was destroyed.

Then I walked into my bedroom. My comic book

collection, shoeboxes full of my baseball cards, was all gone. The laboratory table Dad had made for me for Christmas the year before to hold my chemistry set was badly charred. The P-51 and P-47 model airplanes I'd assembled from kits and hung from the ceiling on strings were unrecognizable lumps of plastic on the floor. I had not shed a tear until that moment.

Sometimes I think about serendipity. Well over half a century later, I think—now and again—about little decisions that don't seem to be important at the time but have consequences far beyond those anticipated. How can we know which decisions those are? We can't.

That fire comes to mind once in a while. My sister and I are incredibly lucky to be here today. We were fortunate that our parents survived. All too often, house fires in our rural communities resulted in a tragic loss of life.

My parents never talked about the night the house burned. The only thing I remember Dad saying about the fire is that he wouldn't call the fire department for a house fire again. It's not that the volunteer fire department did poorly. It was that what was left of the house wasn't really salvageable. If it had burned to the ground, there would have been no question about having to rebuild from a new foundation up.

I wonder if Mom and Dad ever thought about the decision they wrestled with that night, whether or not to send Terrie and me with Grandma Borton to spend the night with her rather than stay at home. Did they both agree with that decision? Did they ever lay awake at night thinking about what could have happened if they had decided to keep us home that night?

That was one of my first steps in coming to understand that every day here on earth is a bonus.

Sailing Down the Channel of Life

IN THE SPRING OF 1965, OUR LIVES CHANGED DRASTICALLY. We were still living in one of cousin Steve Tassier's rental cabins just a quarter-mile up Lakeside Road from our home that had burned. The cleanup of the old house had been completed.

Young Kenny (Boog) Griffin had helped tear down the remains of the roof and walls of the old house. He salvaged the undamaged main floor of the house. My mother marveled at how he had jacked it free of the foundation and with an assortment of hooks, pulleys, and cables, was able to lift it up and swing it over onto his trailer. "He could have been an engineer," she said, shaking her head in awe. That floor became the floor of his new auto shop he'd constructed on the Four Mile Block across the road from "Jerry's Place."

There had been a concern that our insurance coverage might not allow us to replace our house with new construction. The insurance adjuster had visited the place after the fire. Mom and Dad were under the impression that the adjuster believed we had coverage for only $5,000 in damage. They feared the adjuster might evaluate the gutted structure as salvageable, and we might be stuck with having to rebuild using the fire-scarred bones of the old house. The adjuster, however, declared the house a total loss. Mom and Dad were sure he had not known our coverage included damages up to $10,000. As a result of his evaluation, we were able to construct a new home on a new foundation.

That winter, however, Dad broke his leg on the job at Kincheloe AFB, a spiral fracture of both his tibia and fibula bones in his lower leg. While that entitled him to workers' compensation, it did not entirely replace his wages. Nonetheless, we began construction. Dad helped with the construction as best he could, but he was hampered by a cast that encased his left leg from his upper thigh to his toes.

Terrie and I helped where we could. We were eleven and thirteen respectively, so the amount of help we could offer was limited. We did carry "mud" that Dad mixed to Deed Smith, the man who laid the cement block foundation. We didn't need a babysitter. We had Dad, though his skills at watching the kids, never mind his being hobbled, left us a lot of time to play unattended.

Clearing a forested lot for the new house required cutting trees and removing stumps. Remembering the raft we had lashed together at my grandmother's two summers before, I began dragging cedar and balsam logs down to the shore. Access to nails and hammers wasn't a problem.

This raft was going to be different. It wasn't going to be tethered to shore when complete. No, we were going to sail this raft all over Joker Bay and down Moscoe Channel. I constructed a center board from scraps of one-inch boards once I had the raft nailed together.

Dad took a break from overseeing construction of the new house to see what we were doing.

"What's that?" he asked.

"That's going to be our center board for our raft," I said. "We need one, so we'll be able to tack against the wind."

"That won't be big enough," he replied. "That's more of the size you'll need for a rudder."

He helped us build a bigger center board. He figured out how to attach the rudder for steering the raft. Next, he found two skinny poles for the mast and boom. Then, to both of us kids' surprise, he found a scrap of canvas to use for a sail. That it had once been a drop cloth for painting projects didn't make any difference. The green, brown, and white paint splatters on the graying canvas added a pirate character to our project.

When it was completed, Terrie and I pushed our raft out from shore. We had strapped on our orange life jackets. My blue jeans were soaked to the knees, my tennis shoes wet and muddy, but that was not unusual. When we cleared our dock with its varnished mahogany Chris-Craft securely tied under its galvanized tin roof, we hoisted our sail.

I immediately tried to sail crosswind, hoping the centerboard and rudder would allow our raft to tack upwind like a sailboat. Angling the rudder all the way to one side or the other, I could point the raft left or right about forty-five degrees relative to the direction of the wind. The raft, however, refused to change its direction of travel. There was only downwind; there would be no sailing back for us. Like time moving in only one direction, there was no reversing course for Terrie and me.

Out of Joker Bay we sailed. We slid quietly down Moscoe Channel, past the Robley's Sunnyside Resort, past Schurfranz's

Northwind Cabins, past the summer cottages of Down Staters and residents of Ohio, Illinois, and Indiana. As we sailed past the docks, people waved to us and picked up their cameras to photograph the local Huck Finns sailing their log raft.

We sailed downwind, pushed by the steady breeze from the southeast. It might have been rough out on the big lake, but we were buffered from the wind and waves by the islands. With a strong southeast wind, there was a storm coming. My sister and I sailed on, oblivious of that which was behind us or of what was to come.

A half-mile downwind from home, we passed the little rock reef where black terns nested, too near for their comfort. The charcoal gray terns rose up off the reef pumping their sharp-pointed wings. They swooped close and dove at us, calling "ka kew, ka kew, kik, kik, kik," warning us away from their nests and young ones. On we sailed.

At nearly a full mile from home, we realized it was going to take forever to push pole the raft back home. Reluctantly, we lowered our sail and began the not-so-fun task of poling our raft back upwind. A half-hour later, we hadn't made much progress.

Then we heard the throaty roar as a Chris-Craft started up, its pitch rising as it headed in our direction. Dad decided we'd gone far enough and came to tow us home.

Terrie and I continued to sail our raft that summer. Some days we had to sail the quarter-mile down into Joker Bay with the prevailing west wind. On those days, it wasn't far to wade to the shoreline, pulling our raft back home. On days with an east wind when we sailed down Moscoe Channel, Dad would some-times come to our rescue, though it was not guaranteed.

Recalling that summer, it's like turning the raft to a

different orientation. I'm facing another direction, but the wind is still carrying me downwind. Unlike that summer, there won't be a father with a cast on his leg coming to get me with the Chris-Craft.

Mayflies

ONE OF THE EVENTS OF SUMMER we came to count on in the Snows was the mayfly hatch. Each June, mayfly nymphs (we called them "wigglers") emerged from the mud of the lake bottom where they had developed for one to two years. They made their way to the surface of the lake, shed their skins (exoskeletons), and emerged as adults.

During the hatches, yellow perch swarmed in a feeding frenzy. Lake herring would enter the bays and channels from the big lake to gorge on mayflies. Summer fishing peaked as boatloads of tourists filled the bays and channels during the fly hatches, there for the exceptional fishing.

The hatch usually happened at night. Lifting off the water, the adult mayflies would fly to shore, attracted to streetlights and porch lights. I remember being out in a flat-bottomed rowboat on warm June nights, the still air filled with the sounds of frogs and crickets. I leaned out over the bow of the rowboat with my Eveready "Big Jim" six-volt flashlight sitting beside me, its beam angled down into the green water.

On the nights of big hatches, that light would catch mayfly nymphs in the bright green arc of lantern light in the water, rising from the depths like hundreds of tiny mermaids, undulating their way to the surface of the lake. Once in a while, I'd see the flash of a perch or herring in the light as they snatched wigglers just below the surface, minutes before they emerged from their nymphal stage.

Most of them reached the surface. When they did, their exoskeletons split down the back, and a pair of rumpled wings emerged from the old shell. They unfolded slowly until fully extended, and then the rest of the mayfly would appear. There would be a struggle as the adult finally freed itself of its vestiges of youth, abandoning their old skin before—after a pause—when the new adult would spring into the night air. Often the fledgling adult would fly to my boat with the light and land on me. Attaching itself to my shirtsleeve or ball cap, where it joined the other mayflies that had found, in me, their first refuge in adulthood as well as a new environment.

In the morning, we would wake to a world covered in mayflies, their light green bodies sporting wings that lofted vertically. Light poles and trees were often covered by these flies. Sides of buildings would be coated with freshly hatched, light green mayflies. The streets of town were sometimes littered with living mayflies. In the small villages, sidewalks were slick with dead insects crushed under the shoes of pedestrians.

Mayflies are about as harmless as baby birds. Adult mayflies can't bite as they have no functional mouth parts. Neither do they feed. They live for only one or two days as adults, just enough time to molt their exoskeletons once more, to perform mating dances in the sky, and for the female to lay her eggs on the water's surface to begin the cycle anew.

Mayflies made for great bait. We would collect several

hundred in paper bags and store them in the freezer for use later in the summer.

During the winter, mayfly nymphs were the favored bait for ice fishing. One wiggler threaded onto a small Russian teardrop, a hook adorned with a swollen pearl-like shank with a single red dot painted on, was good for one perch, maybe two.

Over the years, the hatches grew less and less abundant. The fishing steadily grew poorer. A lot of people blamed the decline in fish populations on illegal gillnets and overfishing by both tourists and local fishermen.

That wasn't the case. Lakeshores were crowded as more people had built houses on the lake. Every house, every cabin had a septic tank and a drain field downslope. Every drain field extended toward the lake, marked by bright green patches in otherwise non-remarkable lawns. Nutrients seeped into our lake, spurring the growth of undesirable weeds and algae. Water quality was affected. The mayflies, some of the most sensitive organisms to pollution, were just the first to go. An environment that couldn't support mayflies couldn't support healthy fish populations. Over the years, the fly hatch waned. They never disappeared, but it was nothing like "the old days."

In the early 1960s, the Township Board decided that a sewer system was needed, not necessarily because of the decline in mayflies, but because the shallow waters around our towns were becoming weed-choked. Fishing suffered. Water quality declined. If we had been attentive, we would have realized that the entire cycle had been predicted by the mayflies.

The sewer was to be funded by bonds. The bonds would be paid back through property taxes applied township-wide. We didn't own property on the water. Our sewer wasn't affecting water quality. You might think that a sewer system meant to clean up the waters upon which our towns depended for their livelihood, their recreation, would be a no-brainer. Not so. My parents were opposed to the project.

"It's going to raise our property taxes," they complained. Not only that, while the plan called for the sewer collection system to run down every road in the township, but home-owners along the system would also be responsible for the cost of running their sewer lines to the road. Adding to this, each home-owner would be charged an additional $800 for connecting their sewers with the township's.

We didn't have $800 in the bank. Minimum wage was around $1 per hour. Mom and Dad worked only 3,000 hours per year between them. Any costs in addition to income, social security, property, and sales taxes would put us in a difficult place. I didn't understand it at the time, but our family was living below the poverty level.

The bond issue failed. The fly hatches continued to decline.

When I reached high school several years later, I was looking for ways to supplement my meager summer employment income. In 1968, I teamed up with Randy Dunn, a friend who lived a hundred yards up the road, and my cousin Dale Griffin, to dig wigglers during the winter and sell them for bait.

Randy's older brother Dale and his friend Ralph had dug wigglers for several years and had a system for doing it. Randy had access to some of the equipment they used: the end of a fifty-five-gallon drum cut down to a tray only four inches deep and a framed screen to set on top of the tray. Tangles of aquatic weeds, wigglers, and mud could be placed on the screen, and with a heat lamp above, the wigglers would burrow down through the weeds, through the screen and drop into an inch of water in the tray.

Guy Plank welded a one-foot cube from a half-inch reinforcing rod with an iron lip on one edge attached to a tube into which we could insert a tamarack handle. He tacked hardware cloth around the whole basket. I think it cost me ten dollars, but even in the late Sixties, that was a bargain. Randy's father, Archie, told me we needed a tamarack handle for our wiggler scoop. Tamarack was heavy, but it was *strong*. We found a tree that was tall and skinny, about three inches in diameter, and cut it for our handle. We inserted the thick end into the iron tube on the scoop, drove a 16-penny nail through it, and clinched it over to lock it in.

We started next to the Patrick's Landing dock in about six feet of water. We used an axe, to begin with. Unfortunately, when we would get to the bottom of the ice, inevitably, the hole would fill with water. Our last several minutes of chopping would result in us getting wet, chopping out the last of the ice through ten inches or more of water. Eventually, we graduated to a heavy iron spud, so there was a lot less splashing.

Bruce Patrick took pity on us and loaned us a one-person cedar saw converted to an ice saw. It was about four feet long with a six-inch-wide blade and a wooden handle on one end. He had used it to cut ice blocks in the winter. Those blocks of ice were stored in sawdust-insulated ice houses for use in the summer as refrigeration or by local commercial fishing businesses to preserve their catch. The use of that saw made our work much easier.

It took us a while to figure things out. We had to chop two

holes at opposite corners of an imaginary rectangle, insert the saw, then saw one side of the rectangle, then another, go to the next hole on the far corner, and continue to saw until we met the previous saw cut. It took only one hole to realize we needed to angle the top of our saw inward toward our intended hole so we could push the cake of ice under water and slide it away. If we canted the saw even a little outward, the cake of ice couldn't be jammed through, and we would have to chop the block into smaller pieces to either scoop out or push under. We also learned to shove the cake of ice opposite the direction where we were planning our next hole. Having to cut a hole through a double layer of ice was something we learned to avoid after making just one mistake.

Once our hole in the ice was completed, we lowered the scoop and angled it away from the hole as far as the handle would allow. Then applying upward pressure on the handle against the ice to get the scoop to dig into the mud, we dragged the scoop back toward the hole, collecting a basketful of mud and aquatic weeds. When the handle was vertical, we pulled the scoop to the surface and lowered the handle.

At that point, we began swishing the scoop back and forth in the hole, washing out the mud. After several minutes we dumped the contents on the ice adjacent to the hole and eagerly poked around in the mass of weeds looking for wigglers. A good scoop would average about thirty-five wigglers and take about fifteen minutes to process.

If the weather wasn't too cold, we separated the wigglers from the weeds there on the ice. When it was bitterly cold, we would dump the contents into five-gallon buckets on our sled. We would haul our buckets up the hill to my house. There I had a set up in our well pit under the house. I would dump the weeds onto the screen above the tray and turn on the heat lamp. By morning, all the wigglers would have worked their way out of the weeds and dropped into the tray.

There the wigglers could be counted and sorted. One dozen wigglers were gently lifted from the tray with a fork and transferred into empty half-pint waxed milk cartons (courtesy of the school lunch program). We sold each milk carton and its dozen wigglers to gas station owners who would resell them to ice fishermen for twenty-five cents. The only way to make money in the wiggler digging business was volume.

After a day of counting and sorting wigglers, I would go to bed, shut my eyes, and see pans full of wigglers swimming before me as I counted them out one by one with a fork. We continued digging wigglers for several winters, but we finally quit when our harvest of wigglers declined below the margin of profitability.

In the late Sixties, the sewer project was approved and eventually constructed. One by one, the old, failed septic fields that drained directly into the lake were rendered inoperative. Not long ago, I asked some childhood friends (and *their* kids) about the status of the mayfly hatch. "It's back," they said and sent me photos to prove it. It took years, but the fly hatch recovered, as did the perch fishing.

Other problems with water quality and invasive species have beset the Great Lakes. Overcoming one problem leaves others to be focused upon. In this case, however, the right approach solved this one problem. I often think about the mayfly hatch and water quality, how a solution to resolve the problem had been proposed, and why it had been opposed. There might be a lesson in there for all of us.

Winter Sport

WHEN RANDY, DALE, AND I WERE MAKING EXTRA MONEY digging wigglers, we were looking for ways to have some wintertime fun that didn't cost us a lot of money. Randy had told us about his older brothers Art and Dale, and their friend Ralph, who used to sled down through Patrick's Landing from the road all the way down and onto the lake ice.

Bruce hauled logs off Marquette Island with a horse and dray. He iced down the ruts where the runners of the dray rode maybe five feet apart. In between the iced lanes, the snow was chewed up by the horse's hooves and littered with nuggets of horse manure.

What the boys discovered was that each lane was just perfect for riding their Flexible Flyer™ sleds down the hill side by side. They were also close enough to reach over and try to knock the other guy off the sled or cause him to career off the path, maybe even into the manure lane between them.

As it was, there was a pretty sharp turn in the dray's path as it left the lake and began up the hill. Usually, if they made it that far without being thrown off the sled, that last turn usually had them flying over the berm where boy and sled would crash after a moment airborne. Apparently, it was good sport despite the fact no one was ever seriously harmed.

When Randy, Dale, and I were thinking about this, Bruce was no longer hauling timber off the island, so we had no readily available track to jump on. But we had another idea.

Just down the hill and across the road from our house on the corner was the Spring Lodge, owned by the Collins family. Late each autumn, they locked up the Lodge for winter and spent the season in Florida. They generally returned in April to re-open the Lodge and its many cottages for tourists who came in the summer to fish the Les Cheneaux.

The Spring Lodge was named for its spring that ran year-round. The Collinses had corralled the spring in a box on the side of the hill halfway down to the lake. From there, a steady flow of water splashed out of a pipe into an open wooden box sunk into the ground before being collected again and chan-neled into minnow tanks alongside the Spring Lodge boathouse.

The spring ran all year. If us kids got hot and thirsty playing baseball or yard hockey, we would traipse down past the Lodge, kneel beside the spring, and drink deeply of the cool water from the pipe.

Dad told me that my grandmother would rise before dawn on Easter to fill a pitcher of spring water at sunrise. She claimed that was holy water. Other people used the spring as a water source.

Dad's friend since childhood, Dave Mandoskin, would fill a five-gallon milk can every few days from the Spring Lodge spring and trudge back up the hill with it when the gate was closed. Dave didn't have running water. In the winter, he parked along the road and carried his can up and down a trail he'd packed between the road and the spring.

We figured that the spring was a nice supply of water, and we would use it to create our own icy track from the road all the way down to the lake. Only we weren't going to use sleds. Oh, no. Our ice track would be so narrow we were going to strap on ice skates to run it.

It took several days, but eventually, we packed down the snow and iced it all down. We even built a jump, a ramp a couple of feet high just at the bottom of the hill at a point where a guy might have achieved what we thought of as "terminal velocity," a speed nearly impossible to exceed. We'd watch and see how far a guy could fly through the air and whether or not he could stick the landing and make it all the way to the lake.

It was a lot more difficult than we imagined. Those short little skate blades were easily turned off the trail by bumps in the ice. We persisted, however, and fixed the worst spots with more snow and ice. Eventually, we were making it from the road, gaining speed down past the Lodge, whipping past the spring, down onto the jump... and then it was flailing arms and knees and a crash. I don't remember any of us ever making the jump and coasting all the way down to the lake.

Unfortunately, it all came to an end one day in March.

Dad pulled me aside. "Don't ice down the trail anymore," he said.

One night Dave had pulled up on the side of the road, stepped onto the trail with his five-gallon milk can, and... *Whoosh.* He told Dad he was doing OK as he passed the Lodge and then the spring, but he hit the jump on his back and came down hard. He slid past the minnow tanks and made it all the way to the lake.

It didn't occur to us that we could have started to ice down another trail parallel to the original, but winter was almost over anyways. The Collins family would be returning and plowing all the roads. It was time to move on and think about trout fishing and camping.

Fool's Mate

IN JUNIOR HIGH SCHOOL, I WENT OUT FOR BASKETBALL, not because I was a gifted athlete but because of the cheerleaders. Oh, we had some remarkable girls on the cheer squad: Marcie, Pam, Jill, Debbie, and Roseanne. What better way to get close to them than to join the team and ride the team bus to the away games?

At one of our first practices, Coach had us doing one-on-one defensive drills. One player was given the ball and would try to drive to the basket while the other player defended. Coach put me up against probably the best guard on our team, Fred. Fred could dribble the basketball with either hand without even looking at the ball. He could shoot or pass with either hand. Fred was our team's equivalent of "Pistol Pete" Maravich. [Author's note: You kids ought to look up "Pistol Pete."]

Coach gave a toot on his chrome whistle to start the drill. Fred confidently dribbled the ball on the hard tile floor that was our gym, approaching me standing on the foul line. I was in my low defensive crouch, arms wide, on the balls of my feet, waiting for Fred to make his move. He jerked his head to my right and drove toward the basket. I scuttled like a crab to my right, blocking his path to the basket and hoping to maybe even swipe the basketball. Yeeaahh. No.

I was looking at nothing but empty basketball court. Fred had switched the ball to his other hand and sped in the other direction. I'd gone for the fake. I whirled around just in time to see Fred put in a layup off the backboard. As he rebounded the ball, Coach hollered at me. "Griffin, you might be a genius with the books, but you sure as hell can't defend your basket."

Fred dribbled the ball past me, giving me a little shoulder bump and a sideways look. "Genius with the books," he said through a smirk. Thanks, Coach.

Fred and I weren't friends. He was confident, good-looking, and athletic. He was cool. Girls hung around him. Me? I was just the opposite. The only thing I seemed to attract was scorn when it came to sports. I did happen to be a good student. I rarely caused trouble in class, but when I did, all it took was a stern look from the teacher to set me straight. Teachers liked me. That didn't help outside the classroom.

I was not a gifted athlete, something that Coach had pointed out. We speculated that his philosophy must have been honed during a career in the Marines where we suspected that he'd been a drill instructor. There was no mercy in his character for the skinny, the chubby, the ungainly. The other kids picked up his uncharitable attitude. Wonderful.

"Genius with the books." That particular taunt hung on for a while before dying out. That was the last year I played basketball. Instead, I took up chess. My cousin Dan taught me how to play one summer. Up until then, I'd been a checkers guy. Checkers was a pretty simple game. All the pieces were the same, and they moved the same way until your checker reached the far side of the board and became a "king" ("Crown me!"). Chess, however, was complicated. There were six different pieces, each with its own rules for movement. The knight moved horizontally or vertically two squares, then diagonally one square that allowed it to "jump" other pieces. But Dan was patient, and I was a quick learner, so we had a good time playing that summer.

One day that fall, I was sitting quietly in study hall, not doing anything except daydreaming. Our new principal, George Truckey, happened by.

"Hmmm... shouldn't you be doing your homework?" he asked.

"All done," I said.

"How about reading your book?"

"I finished it about twenty minutes ago," I responded.

He looked at me, skepticism etched in the corners of his smile. "Well, did you get straight A's last semester?" he asked slowly, figuring he had me.

"Yes, sir, I did." He rolled his eyes and gave me an exasperated look.

"Well, you really need to be doing something in study hall besides staring off into space."

I brought my chess set to study hall and started playing with a friend. Mrs. Becker, who was responsible for study hall, discouraged that, maybe not so much for my playing games in study hall, but I was playing with kids who really could have been using the time to catch up on class work. I put the chessboard away.

My friend and I, being clever high school students, decided to play without a board, to play on paper, each of us recording our moves in two columns. This went slowly, having to visualize what the board looked like and where each of the pieces was. We'd push the paper back and forth when our moves were completed, and that attracted the attention of Mrs. Becker, who was a lot brighter than we had given her credit for. We were dragged into the principal's office. No more chess games in study hall.

I started playing chess at lunchtime in the study hall with several other kids. It was a lot more fun than shooting baskets in the gym, where most of the high school boys congregated after lunch until the bell rang for the first afternoon class.

One of the benefits of being a Boy Scout was *Boy's Life* magazine. Every other issue had a column on chess by a guy by the name of Bobby Fisher. He wrote tips for playing games and featured a puzzle each month: a chess board with several pieces from each side with a note that white was next to move and checkmate black in three moves. It was up to the reader to figure out how that played out. The answer would be published in the next issue.

Readers' questions were also answered. One question from a reader regarded whether or not to use the "Fool's Mate" on opponents. I had never heard of the Fool's Mate. I looked it up and found that it was a way to checkmate your opponent in only four moves. Bobby Fisher said that it was a gimmick and that if you could spring that on your opponent, you would beat him in a normal game played without gimmicks. He advised that's probably what any player should do because no one ever learns anything by checkmating an opponent in four moves.

I couldn't get past the idea of defeating an opponent in four moves. Bobby Fisher's advice to not use gimmicks in a serious game was lost on me.

"Hokey smokes!" I thought, "a checkmate in four moves?" In the school library, I found a chess book that detailed the exact moves needed to checkmate an opponent in four moves. I couldn't wait to try it on an opponent.

At lunch one day, Fred, the basketball player, challenged me to a game. I moved first, advancing the pawn in front of my king out two spaces. Fred matched my move, blocking my king's pawn from further advancing.

For my second move, I advanced my king's bishop diagonally three spaces putting it evenly ranked with my king's pawn. Fred matched my move, so our bishops faced one another in the middle of the board just as our pawns did. This was just like they showed it in the book.

My third move was my queen out diagonally to the right four spaces all the way to the right side of the board, threatening the pawn that defended Fred's king. I held my breath. There were only a couple of moves Fred could make to immediately escape the four-move trap I had laid, if he recognized the trap at all.

Fred touched several pieces, thinking about his next move. It was obvious he was concentrating on offense and had not recognized checkmate in one more move. Fred moved his queen's pawn out one space to defend the pawn he had previously advanced two spaces. That's the move I needed to see.

Picking up my queen between thumb and forefinger, I moved it to the space occupied by his king's bishop's pawn. In one move I picked up his pawn, pinching it between my little finger and the palm of my hand while settling my queen into its place.

"Checkmate," I said confidently as I swept his pawn off the

board. Fred pursed his lips and studied the board. He touched every one of his pieces trying to either capture my queen or get his king out of check. With a smirk, I explained how each move he tried wasn't legal or would leave his king in check.

"You might be a genius with the basketball, Fred, but you sure as hell can't defend your king!"

Fred stood so fast his plastic-and-metal chair fell over backward. He glared at me thin-lipped, his face an angry mask. I looked up at him but remained seated. He reached back with his right hand as though he was going to take a swing at me. Fred swore and swung his fist. At the last minute, he opened his hand and swept all the chessmen off the board onto the floor, the plastic pieces *tink, tink, tinking* as they bounced across the tile floor. He swiveled abruptly and shouldered his way out of the study hall.

Beating Fred didn't feel as good as I thought it might.

Despite my showing off, chess became a popular thing to do during lunch at school. Our impromptu matches gained enough attention that the school organized a chess tournament at the Purple Flat, our community center. Eight of us entered. I used the Fool's Mate the first game I played. The small crowd tittered at that. My opponent stood up, shaking his head, and walked away. "Next," I said. It was on to round two.

My next opponent had seen my first game and withdrew from the tournament without playing a game. That left me waiting for the championship game.

When my next opponent was determined, I was surprised to see that it was my sister, Terrie. I'd taught her how to play. She'd never beaten me. And this day was not going to be any different. We started the game.

I opened with a variation of my four-move checkmate, disguising it within a different offensive strategy. She was expecting that and didn't fall for it at all. After fifteen moves or so, I figured it was time to just beat her straight up. I began a standard attack. She countered. We traded a couple of pawns. Then a couple of more pieces.

She was not providing me any opening to attack her king. We traded a couple more pieces. After twenty-some moves, I became frustrated. I advanced a pawn, moving it diagonally to an empty square. My sister looked puzzled.

"I need some help," she said to the crowd. "I don't think that's a legal move."

She was right. You can't move a pawn diagonally except to capture another piece. I moved the pawn back and followed it with a legal move. The game proceeded slowly. Finally, I wore her down.

I made one last move. "Check. And mate." I said with relief. It had been the longest game I'd ever played. She looked the board over, contemplating potential moves, and then nodded.

"Congratulations," she said, reaching across the board to shake my hand. There I was—high school chess champion.

I had forgotten about that chess championship until a couple of years ago when my sister reminded me of that game.

Recalling that game and doing some research, I learned some things about chess and some things about myself.

In chess, when a player makes a move and removes his hand from the piece being moved, that turn is done. If it's an illegal move, that player is disqualified. I should have been disqualified at that moment. Instead, I was given credit for something that I had not earned. My sister, Terrie, had actually won the chess tournament, not me.

I learned something else that might have been more important. I was eager to show off my ability to beat people at the chessboard. The nerdy, clumsy kid I had been, the kid that had been goaded into unwinnable fights, had enjoyed humiliating people with trick chess plays. Using the Fool's Mate didn't prove I was any good at chess. Maybe that maneuver was given its name because the only people that would use it, a gimmick, to win a chess match were, in fact, the actual fools.

There is more than one way to bully other people. I wonder if it's possible that we are all potential bullies at some point during our lives.

The Year the Rats Invaded Town

BACK IN THE SIXTIES, IT SEEMED LIKE OUR BIGGEST environmental problem was litter. Our roadsides were covered with newspapers, candy wrappers, and beer cans tossed out the car windows. There was a national effort to stop littering, the Keep America Beautiful campaign. You might recall the famous public service ad that included Iron Eyes Cody dressed as a Plains Indian standing on the side of a highway. A bag of litter tossed from a passing station wagon landed at his feet. As he looked down and then stared into the camera, a tear trickled down his cheek.

Hey, we took that stuff seriously. Roadsides weren't the place for litter, also known as garbage. We had a garbage dump located midway between our two communities in the Les Cheneaux Islands. Folks backed up their pickups to the edge of a hill and pitched their garbage over. At least it was concentrated in one spot and out of sight. It was, however, an awfully smelling place. Occasionally, people set the dump on fire. The resulting smoke smelled worse than the garbage itself. The dump was also teeming with rats.

One of the local sports for some in our community was to take a .22 rifle, several boxes of shells, and drive to the dump at night. There, a group of beer-drinking guys would line up their cars and pickup trucks pointed toward the mound of garbage. On a pre-determined signal, they turned their headlights on all at once and shoot at any rats caught in the open. Some folks who have heard this story were horrified at that prospect for several reasons, but I merely report the facts. Many times, I asked Dad if I could go. The answer was always, "No, you're not old enough."

Eventually, environmental laws were passed. Our township converted the dump to a sanitary landfill where the garbage (now called "solid waste") was covered daily with dirt. What had been a haven for rats was covered with several feet of sand and gravel. It did, though, improve the view and cut down on the stench.

Converting the dump to a landfill was a good thing. Nobody, however, gave a thought to the fact that the rats no longer had a place to live. The enterprising rodents spread out through the woods and into the neighboring communities searching for shelter and food.

We lived in an old house that had belonged to my grandmother. Dad had grown up in this house. It had been constructed well before the advent of rural electrification. An existing back porch had been enclosed and converted to an entryway, an extra bedroom, and an indoor toilet. The old front porch had been removed. Dormers punctuated the roofline and an old brick chimney extended above the peak. Part of the house rested on a fieldstone foundation while the remainder sat on wooden pilings. There were a million places a rat could get into the house with next to no effort.

That winter, rats ran freely all over town. One day our dogs cornered a rat up against the snowbanks and were raising a fuss. Dad had to shoot it. After school one day, we came home to find a rat in our kitchen, hiding behind the stove. Dad promptly dispatched the intruder with his .22 rifle.

I have wondered if my memories were accurate, if anyone else remembered the rats. Like Mark Twin said, "When I was younger, I could remember anything, whether it had happened or not; but my faculties are decaying now, and soon I shall be so I cannot remember any but the things that never happened." So, I asked my friend Art if he remembered the year the rats invaded the town.

"Boy, I'll say," he said. "It was Christmas Eve, and the family was sitting in the living room, the Christmas tree up and decorated, watching TV, when a rat ran across the living room floor and into the master bedroom." Art's Dad, Archie, grabbed a hockey stick and chased after it, slamming the bedroom door behind him.

The rat had sought refuge behind the pile of Christmas presents that were to be placed under the tree after the kids had gone to bed. Archie began handing presents out of the bedroom one at a time as the kids watched. "Hey, look at that one, it's for me. Look at the size of that one!" They heard a *wham, wham, wham.* The rat had run into the closet. Archie began pulling clothes out of the closet until all that was left was one hanger bearing a pair of dress pants *with a large lump in one leg.* Wielding the hockey stick like Paul Bunyan's ax, Archie gave it a two-handed slash that would have earned him a five-minute major penalty and a game misconduct in the NHL, killing the rat. Art's mother, Bernadine, had everything in the house dry cleaned.

Art's younger brother, Randy, had a story as well. Archie had put rat traps in the crawl space under the house. A rat had sprung a trap but wasn't killed, so Archie sent Randy under the house armed with a pump pellet pistol to finish it off. Randy said he got a close as he dared before pulling the trigger, but he missed. The rat charged him, and Randy had to crawl out from under the house backward as fast as he could while trying to reload the one-shot pistol and pump it up.

So, my memory wasn't faulty. Other folks remembered the rat invasion as I did.

With all this going on, I had a recurring dread, one that involved waking up in the middle of the night with a rat in my bedroom. I'd heard terrible stories about babies being bitten by rats in Detroit. I knew rats spread diseases like the bubonic plague. I had an awful feeling about it.

Late one night, long after lights out, I was in my upstairs bedroom of our old house, huddled under the blanket in bed, with my flashlight reading my most recent science fiction discovery, *The Moon Is a Harsh Mistress*. There came a *scratchy* noise, the sound of tiny, sharp claws on the worn pine flooring behind a cardboard box in a darkened corner. I knew what that represented. I laid there, hoping it would go away. It didn't. I pulled the blanket off my head and waved my flashlight around. "Go away, rat!" The noise paused briefly but then continued.

Fear paralyzed me into inaction. I knew that the minute I jumped off the bed and made my way over to the light switch, the rats would be on me. I didn't have a loaded .22 in the bedroom (probably a good thing). I didn't even have a hockey stick handy.

Then I had an idea! I had taken up bow hunting that fall.

Slowly plucking my bow from the bedroom wall, I strung it and nocked my only broadhead, all while keeping the flashlight pointed in the general vicinity of the noise.

I wasn't messing around. It was going to be him or me. Even then, I had a flair for hyperbole. That rat was going to die! I stood there in the middle of my bed in my underwear, hands and knees shaking, trying to keep the flashlight aimed, the shaft of the arrow rattling against the bow.

Out from behind that cardboard box out slunk a hideous animal ... slowly inching out into the light ... a rat nose, followed by rat whiskers, great big beady rat eyes... sleek gray fur, and then ... the tail. Not a skinny, scaly, rat tail... but a broad, flattened, furry tail. It was no rat! It was a flying squirrel!

To me, flying squirrels, up until that moment, lived only as pictures in books. As far as I knew, they were rare and exotic animals. I was about as likely to encounter one of those damned flying monkeys from the *Wizard of Oz*, another source of bad dreams. I didn't even know we had flying squirrels in Upper Michigan.

Well, I wasn't afraid of any squirrel, so I jumped off the bed. The squirrel scurried back into the wall from where it had come. A gap between the floorboards and the wall boards proved to be his access point. I stuffed some dirty socks into the gap and finally felt safe. It was a relief. I reported the fact we had a flying squirrel problem to my parents the next morning.

Dad borrowed some Havahart™ live traps from the Club. We trapped three flying squirrels over the next few nights and released them several miles away.

Flying squirrels are not uncommon, though I suspect that not many folks have laid eyes on one. And despite their name, they don't fly. They glide, aided by flaps of skin between their forelegs and back legs, a lot like ski jumpers who don't fly but glide long distances riding a cushion of air downhill.

These shy little animals den in hollow trees and sometimes use witches' brooms for shelter.

Their diet is varied, and they are described as omnivorous, which means they'll eat just about anything they can get their little paws on, including meat, mushrooms, green vegetation, lichens, seeds, and even birds' eggs and nestlings! They may be cute, but they *are* animals, doing what they must to survive.

What good are flying squirrels? Well, they're an important part of our forests. It seems like everything needs to have some use these days for us to get a sense of its value. Flying squirrels play an important role. They not only serve as food for other animals like goshawks and pine martens, but they also perform a more critical function. Flying squirrels are mycophages, meaning they eat fungi. They dig up the underground fruiting bodies (truffles) of important fungus for food and scatter the fungal spores in their droppings throughout the forest (including clear-cuts or burned areas where there are no fungi).

We tend to think about mushrooms or toadstools when we think of fungi, but these are merely the reproductive features of fungi. The fungi exist mainly in the form of hyphae, thin, branching threads that grow through the soil, in total called the mycelium. The finest of these thin fungal threads measure only the diameter of one cell.

Root hairs of trees are microscopically thin roots branching from the larger tree roots. The finest of these root hairs inter-twine with the mycelia in a symbiotic relationship called a mycorrhiza (these words have Greek origins meaning *fungus* and *root*). Scientists hypothesize that most plant families on the Earth form mycorrhizae.

In this relationship, the fungal mycelia allow the tree to absorb water and nutrients more efficiently, while the rhiza (root hairs) provide starches to its fungal partner. In some relationships, the fungus produces antibiotics that protect the tree roots from diseases, and others produce nematocides, chemicals that kill nematodes that feast on plant roots.

In places where mycorrhizae exist, trees grow better, faster, and in greater health. They out-compete their neighbors that may not have the benefit of mycorrhizae. To claim there would be no trees without flying squirrels would be an exaggeration. But without flying squirrels, there might be fewer trees that don't grow as well. Is the flying squirrel important? I think so.

Later in life, I encountered flying squirrels many times, especially around cabins in the woods and often while deer hunting early in the morning. They are observable in that gray time that's not quite night but still a nice long nap before sunup. In that time, I would often hear scrambling of tiny, clawed feet and a dim streak across my path, ending with a plop on a standing snag near my deer stand. Just another flying squirrel arriving home for the night as my day was starting.

Years after earning a degree in biology from Lake Superior State, I learned about Professor Barry Commoner's four laws of ecology: everything is connected; everything has to go somewhere, there is no free lunch, and nature knows best.

Everything is connected.

You can't do one thing without affecting something else. We could cover the dump, but that had another effect.... The rats moved out.

• **Everything has to go somewhere.**

Our garbage never just "goes away."

• **There is no free lunch.**

There's a cost to dealing with our waste, though sometimes not a direct dollar cost.

• **Nature knows best.**

I've always had a problem with this one. If nature knows best, those of us who wear glasses, who've ever had an inflamed appendix removed before it ruptures, or who can still point to a Smallpox vaccination scar on our shoulder, have seemingly thwarted nature's will.

Eventually, I've come to interpret the phrase, "nature knows best," as a reminder that—in nature—nothing ever goes to waste. Nature doesn't have garbage dumps *or* sanitary landfills. Everything is used up one way or another or recycled. And that's something we can remember to emulate in nature. Reduce our garbage, re-use what we can, and recycle the rest.

When I talk to kids about natural history and ecosystems and how everything is tied together, I tell them my story about the year the rats invaded town.

Summer Work

IN THE SUMMER OF 1967, our family had just returned to Cedarville from a nine-month stay in Oregon. We had moved to Molalla the previous fall as Dad looked for work. It was an interesting experiment. My sister and I saw country we had previously only seen in magazine pictures. Soon our grandmother (Dad's mother) was in a nursing home in St. Ignace, immobilized and speechless due to a stroke, so family responsibilities called us back to Cedarville.

I was now fifteen years of age. Summers between school years no longer required babysitters. There would be no more playing in the woods. I needed to find summer work. At first, I found problems looking for work while still under the age of sixteen. Legally, I couldn't operate machinery, so there wasn't much chance of being hired by any boat shops, gas stations, or construction companies.

I could, however, mow lawns. My cousin Dave and his family had just moved into town from their house near the Four Mile Block on the upland side of the road paralleling the Snow Channel. The lake side of the street was dominated by "cottages" squeezed into 100-foot lots along the lake, each with its own dock and boathouse to shelter their varnished mahogany Chris-Crafts. "Summer people" were folks who lived Down Below—The Detroit metroplex, Ohio, or Indiana—who could afford to spend their summers Up North out of the heat and humidity. They all had lawns to be manicured and flower gardens to weed but no time to tend them. When Dave moved into town, he was no longer available for his mowing business, and he passed his customers on to me.

Because Dave now lived too far away to tend those lawns, I was in the perfect place to take over his lawn mowing circuit. Lugging a one-gallon can of gas, I pushed my lawn mower down the road, turning off onto the gravel driveways of my clients, down toward their cottages on the lake. Based on advice from Dave, I charged one dollar and fifty cents per lawn and one dollar and twenty-five cents per hour for any work assigned other than cutting the grass. Those folks would have me raking leaves, trimming with grass shears around cabins and rock gardens where the mower couldn't reach. Depending on the weather and the amount of rain received, I revisited those lawns every ten to fourteen days.

I was paid in cash after every job. After my very first afternoon mowing lawns, I stopped at the Snows Bar on the way home, parked my lawnmower outside the door, and bought a six-pack of Coke. That cold Coke, the bottle dripping condensation, purchased with my own hard-earned money, was the best Coke I ever drank. It was almost like I was an adult.

About mid-summer, we were visited by Bruce, the owner of Patrick's Landing. His lakeside resort and boat shop were located just down the road. One of his friends, Jim Anderson, a summer cottage owner, was looking for help with yard mainte-nance. Bruce mentioned my name to Jim as he thought I might be interested. I was.

The next day I walked across the road to the Anderson place. Two fieldstone pillars guarded the gravel driveway, which led to a deep-green two-story house with white trim and many windows. I passed a fenced enclosure with a kennel and a Labrador retriever that displayed some interest in me but did not bark. I knocked on the back door and was met by a man in his late fifties or early sixties, balding with light gray, blond hair, his lined face sporting wire-rimmed glasses. That was Jim.

Jim and his wife Jeanne were retired and had long been summer residents of the Les Cheneaux Islands. Jeanne was a pleasant woman with a large smile, high cheekbones, and kind eyes behind thick-lensed glasses. Their home was in Cincinnati, but they spent more than six months per year Up North at the cottage.

Jim mentioned that his brother, John, had won the 1932 Olympics gold medal in shot put. Of course, when I got home, I looked up the 1932 Olympics in the *World Almanac* I'd received for Christmas. This thick paperback book contained a wealth of information, a place to go for facts before there was an internet. Sure enough, the 1932 Olympic Games were held in Los Angeles, and the gold medal winner for shot put was John Anderson.

Jim walked me around the place, showing me the property lines up to which I would mow. A screened porch ran the length of the lake side of the house. Stone walls contained raised flower beds choked with quack grass in front. A flagstone path led from the front steps down to a cedar crib dock with a dark green clapboard boat house roofed with gray shingles.

Peeking into the boathouse, I saw a twenty-four-foot white

fiberglass inboard/outboard named *Missy*, after the Andersons' granddaughter. Alongside it was an eighteen-foot Boston Whaler with a stout Johnson motor on the stern. One of my responsibilities would be to clean up the barn swallow droppings off the boats as there were several families of swallows nesting in the boathouse rafters. Jim was too much of an environmentalist to knock the nests down after eggs had been laid.

We settled on a schedule that had me working three half-days per week. I cut grass. I trimmed around the rock gardens and along the flagstone path to the boat house. I cleaned up the boats. Eventually, Jeanne had me spade up the front gardens, which had been neglected for several years. That job took me the better part of a day, turning the sod and raking out the long quack grass roots. I planted Jeanne's latest flower purchases from The Green Thumb, our local greenhouse. The Andersons appreciated my work. Jim wrote me a check every Friday, buck-and-a-quarter an hour.

What I didn't splurge on Cokes went into my savings account at the bank, each entry typed into my passbook and initialed by the teller. College was going to be awfully expensive, and I knew my parents wouldn't be able to help me out much financially.

One of my tasks that summer was to feed the Labrador retriever, Lady. She had just given birth to a litter of pups and was entitled to a special diet. I mixed her food with scientific precision. First, there was the kibble, a fancy dog food not named *Purina*. I mixed that with a half can of Alpo. I added an egg. The last ingredient was a powder made especially for lactating dogs, along with a couple of cups of warm water. As instructed, I mixed all this up by hand in the kitchen and served

Lady in the pen with her pups.

To be sure, this wasn't how our dog at home ate. Barney, our beagle, got a couple of cups of Purina dog food every day. He didn't get any special additives except for scraps off the dinner plates, not that there were many of those. Barney was an under-privileged dog, I guess.

In the summer of 1968, I officially entered the job market. I had turned sixteen that winter which meant I could be formally hired by a business and operate power equipment, though I had to have a work permit signed off by the high school principal. I was hired by the Les Cheneaux Club to mow lawns on their extensive holdings on the Club Point on Marquette Island. Three days per week, Dad and I would drive down to the Club Dock at the golf course to catch the ferry at 7:30 a.m. for the half-mile ride to the Club Dock on the island side. Dad was one of a crew of a half dozen men and two or three kids my age employed by the Club, an association of well-to-do summer cottage owners from Down Below: Ohio, Indiana, and Illinois. They were owners and heirs of some of the country's biggest companies, including Armour, Eli Lily, and Sears and Roebuck, who spent summers in the Les Cheneaux with their families.

Despite my work with the Club, I continued working for Jim Anderson, three half-days per week when I wasn't working at the Club. My work with Jim grew beyond yard work. One of my tasks, once I earned my driver's license, was to haul the Anderson's trash to our local garbage dump. The dump was located just off the "Blind Line," a gravel road that had once linked the communities of Hessel and Cedarville until construction of a state highway that followed the lake shore from the Straits of

Mackinac through Cedarville and Hessel all the way to DeTour (now known as "DeTour Village" to avoid confusion) at the eastern end of the Upper Peninsula.

Once a week, I loaded two or three trash cans into Jim's pea-soup-green station wagon and went to the dump. One day, returning from the weekly dump trip, I pulled into the Anderson's driveway, but I didn't take the corner wide enough. Before I realized my mistake, there was a horrifying "skreeuunnchhh!" as the passenger side of the car scraped past the fieldstone pillar.

Oh no! I jumped out of the car and looked over the damage. The passenger door was deeply creased, and several patches of Bondo™ had sheared off. Bondo? Bondo was a filler used to patch up and smooth out dings and dents in cars. Apparently, something like this had happened before.

That was little comfort, though. This kind of damage would easily run several hundred dollars to repair. If I didn't lose my job outright, I'd be working a long time to pay for it. Resigned, I pulled the car down next to the house. I went in and told Jim what had happened.

We went out into the driveway and looked at the car. I hung my head. "It was my fault," I said. "I'll pay to get it fixed."

"No," Jim said, shaking his head, "we'll just chalk this up to experience."

I kept my job.

The Trial of Stone Castle's Yellow Jacket

In the summer of 1968, Jim's retriever, Lady, was as much a family pet as a hunting companion. Jim had acquired a new Labrador retriever, Stone Castle's Yellow Jacket. Stoney was a registered and professionally trained three-year-old yellow Lab. Jim had a training regimen to keep Stoney in shape, not only for duck season but also for competition in field trials.

Several days a week, we would take Stoney to some open fields owned by friends of Jim several miles north on the Rock View Road. I would stand away from Jim and his dog by thirty yards or so and throw the dummy by its short rope handle. They would watch to see where it landed. Then Jim would lean down toward his dog, sharply command "back," in combination with a hand signal in the direction of the dummy, the sign for Stoney to break from Jim's side to retrieve the dummy.

We also practiced double retrieves. Jim would throw one dummy from his position next to Stoney, and I, from several yards away, would use a device powered by a blank .22 caliber cartridge to launch another dummy forty or fifty yards away from the first dummy thrown. Jim would then direct Stoney to retrieve the first dummy. After the first dummy was retrieved,

Jim would have Stoney sit again before sending him out on a line with the second dummy I had launched. It was a test of Stoney's ability to recall where the second dummy fell, his ability to "mark" its fallen position.

Jim's confidence in Stoney's abilities grew that summer, to the point he decided to use live birds for training. Jim purchased several pheasants from a local pheasant farm. This was going to be a bigger production than normal, so Jim enlisted some help. In addition to me, he invited Karl, one of Jim's long-time friends from Cincinnati, and Ralph, Bruce's nineteen-year-old son from the boat shop.

We went to the fields on Rock View Road. The plan was to have me release pheasants by tossing them in the air. Once the pheasant flew far enough, Ralph or Karl would shoot it. Then Jim would have Stoney retrieve the dead bird, under conditions somewhat similar to actual pheasant hunting, but virtually the same as Stoney would encounter in American Kennel Club-sanctioned field trials Jim planned to enter.

In the field, we all got out of our vehicles and watched while Jim pulled a crate with two pheasants out of the back of his green station wagon onto the tail gate. Karl and I stood near him and watched as Jim opened the crate door, reaching inside to grab one of the nervous birds. Jim was inside the crate up to his arm pit trying to corral a bird and finally caught one by a leg. He dragged the bird out, cradling it to his chest, trying to get a better grip on it, when the pheasant, sensing an opportunity for freedom, burst from Jim's hold in a wild flapping of wings and shower of feathers. It gained speed and flew directly away from us, its bid for freedom almost assuredly a success.

Jim barely had time to say, "Well, that's gone," when our

disappointment was interrupted by a shotgun blast. The bird, about three seconds into its flight to freedom, crumpled and fell into the short grass. Stunned, we whirled around and looked at Ralph. A slow grin spread across his face. He lowered his double-barreled Parker shotgun, broke it open, and a spent shell popped out.

Stoney had not left Jim's side. Jim squared himself to where the pheasant had fallen, crouched next to the yellow Lab, and uttered the command, "back" with the attending hand signal. Stoney broke for the bird on a dead run. He grabbed it and returned, laying the dead bird at Jim's feet. "Good boy," he said, rumpling the happy dog's ears.

Later, when we were done for the day, I asked Ralph what had made him load his shotgun as soon as we had arrived at the field. He looked at me, that slow grin of his growing once again. "That's not the first time that's happened," he smiled.

My yard work and dog training with Jim continued into the fall. One day in early October, Jim asked me if I would be available to help him run Stoney in a field trial somewhere down on the Flat River in the Lower Peninsula. "I was going to enter Lady in the trial, too, but she's in estrous."

I must have had a puzzled look on my face. "She's in season," he said.

When the blank look on my face persisted, Jim said, "She's in heat," with a note of mild exasperation, before his meaning finally dawned on me.

"Oh. In heat," I said. In estrous? I'd never heard that term before.

This field trial was a competition for retrievers, including Labrador retrievers, Chesapeake Bay retrievers, and golden retrievers as well. It was a four-hour trip from Cedarville and would include staying at motels Friday and Saturday nights.

Jim said he wouldn't pay me twenty-four hours per day but asked if I thought ten dollars was reasonable. I was no slouch at math. That meant pay at one dollar and twenty-five cents per hour for eight hours per day for three days, a total of thirty dollars.

I checked with my parents. They were fine with me taking off for a weekend with Jim.

We left on a Friday afternoon after school, Jim's green station wagon full of dog crate, training dummies, dog food, and one wide-eyed kid with an overnight bag. Over to St. Ignace we drove, crossed the Mackinac Bridge, and then headed south on I-75.

We pulled into a motel late that evening in a small town near the field trial grounds. The next morning, we visited a restaurant where I had blueberry pancakes dripping with blue-berry-flavored syrup for breakfast. I recall them being the best pancakes I'd ever eaten outside my grandmother's house. At home, Mom and Dad favored buckwheat pancakes. Buckwheat pancakes were only tolerable—to my taste, anyway.

Jim registered with the folks running the field trail. We watched a few of the young dogs in the first competition, the Derby class. That was for dogs that hadn't reached their second birthday. Jim shook his head at one of the entrants, a young golden retriever that was bouncing all over the field in its efforts to locate a fallen bird. It wasn't doing well, but it appeared to be having fun.

"I've always thought golden retrievers to be the dumbest of the retrievers," he said with disgust. "The bench people have ruined that breed," he added.

"What do you mean, *bench people?*" I asked.

"There are two competing groups of people regarding purebred dogs," he said. "The bench crowd breeds dogs for their looks ... whatever dog wins their shows gets bred to reflect those traits they believe look the best for whatever breed of dog they're looking at. They don't breed for performance because performance doesn't win shows. As a result, performance is bred right out of those lines."

Jim grimaced. "As long as a dog looks good and wins shows, it doesn't matter whether it knows a duck from a squirrel or how stupid it is."

"And what are the other people doing?" I asked.

"The field people breed their dogs for performance. They want them to be good hunting dogs, and they measure that by these field trials." We walked back toward the parking lot to get Stoney out of his wire kennel in the back of the green station wagon.

"Not that the field people are perfect either," Jim added. "On a water trial, the judges want your dog to head on a straight line between you and the downed bird, even if it takes longer than the dog running along the bank to get as close to the bird as possible before going in the water. That's what a smart dog does, but they don't judge a dog by how smart it is. That's too hard to measure, so they deduct points if the dog runs the bank on a water retrieve."

In a few minutes we were back, waiting next to the "retrieving line" where the next class of the competition was to begin. Jim and Stoney were one of the earliest pairs. They intently watched the field from behind the retrieving line. The "flier," a pheasant, was released at the line. It flew thirty yards before being dropped by the "gunner." Stoney didn't move. At a blind about fifty yards away, a dead pheasant was thrown into the field, and at the high point in its arc, a "bird boy" fired a blank shotgun shell to attract Stoney's attention.

Jim directed Stoney to retrieve the first bird that had been killed. The dog went straight to the fallen bird and returned to Jim with it, set it at his feet, and then sat waiting for instructions. Jim leaned over his dog, gestured toward the location of the second bird with the flat of his hand, and gave the command, "back." Jim had told me that Stoney was good at marking birds. He had a good memory for areas where birds had fallen. And he had a good nose. Conditions in the field were damp but not soaked with rain, and that favored dogs with good noses. Stoney found and retrieved the second bird without a problem and returned to Jim's side.

Jim was very pleased with Stoney's performance. We put Stoney back in his wire kennel and returned to watch a few other competitors. There were black Labs, other yellow Labs, Chesapeake Bay retrievers, and even the occasional golden retriever. Maybe I was biased, but I noticed every mistake made by the goldens.

Shortly, we were back at the retrieving line. The next trial was a water retrieve. Wanting to get a little closer to the field rather than watch from the retrieving line, I wandered down to the gallery. There I ducked between people to find a place to stand in front of the small crowd near the water.

A dead bird was thrown from the shore, and a bird boy fired his blank. Jim sent Stoney racing down the slight rise from the retrieving line. He made a magnificent leap from the shore into the water. He must have been in the air for ten feet before sending up a huge splash. Stoney paddled straight for the dead bird, ignoring the decoys, grabbed the bird, and headed for shore. He came ashore in a slightly different place than he had entered, a little off the straight line Jim had told me the judges wanted to see.

Stoney came up the slight bank, bird in mouth. As he cleared the bank, he and I made eye contact. Then, he took a faltering step toward me.

"OH, NO," I screamed to myself, "NO, NO, NO!" Stoney never took more than that one slight misstep in my direction. He turned slightly and headed back to Jim on a dead run. I was sure I had screwed up. Nobody in the gallery knew that I knew the dog, so maybe it wasn't obvious Stoney had faltered in his retrieve. But I knew.

Jim was pretty pleased with Stoney's retrieve. He didn't know I was in the gallery. Maybe he hadn't noticed Stoney's brief moment of indecision.

The last trial was a blind retrieve. In a blind retrieve, an official places a dead bird about a hundred yards from the retriever line before the dog comes to the line. The handler is allowed to see where the bird is placed. From the retriever line the handler then guides the dog to the bird using a whistle and hand signals.

The whistle gets the dog's attention, and the handler directs the dog, right, left, in, or back to the area where the bird lays. A successful blind retrieve uses as few whistles and hand signals as possible. The perfect blind retrieve is when the handler directs the dog on a perfect line directly to the bird, but that rarely happens.

What sometimes happens is that a dog, not finding the bird, "pops," sitting and looking back at the handler, waiting for additional direction but before the handler blows the whistle. "Popping" results in a loss of points.

Jim went to the retriever line and told me to keep Stoney back because he didn't want the dog to see the field and maybe get confused. But I wanted to see where they placed the dead bird, so I kept myself between the dog and the field and behind some low bushes that also obscured Stoney's view. I turned the dog to sit facing away from the field as well, but looking over my shoulder, I could see what was going on. After the bird was placed, Jim came back to fetch the dog. He was upset to find me so close to the retriever line and reiterated that he didn't' want the dog confused. I assured him that Stoney hadn't seen a thing, but I know Jim wasn't satisfied. It was just one more screw-up on my part.

Jim set Stoney out on a good line, but at 100 yards, the dog was off by five to ten yards. When Stoney was directly abreast of the bird, he slowed, and Jim blew the whistle. Stoney stopped, turned to look at Jim, and sat, waiting for a hand signal. Jim gave an exaggerated leftward movement with his hand and body. The dog immediately went to the left and, within a few seconds, was on the scent and had the bird in his mouth. He raced back to the retriever line. Yet another good retrieve for Jim and Stoney.

Later Jim told me he believed Stoney was about to "pop" when he blew the whistle. Luckily, the dog was on a direct line when Jim decided he'd best blow the whistle before the dog looked back for direction.

Our part in the field trial was done. We watched some more of the blind retrieves. No dog did as well as Stoney had.

One golden retriever joyously bounced all over the course and, despite multiple whistles, never did find the dead bird. Its handler finally just gave up and called the dog back to the retriever line.

At the end of the day, Jim and I headed back to the motel. We had dinner and then an early lights-out. Late Sunday morning, we gathered in the parking lot of a nearby motel. There were several tables of hors d'oeuvres laid out. I recall a pile of raw hamburger sprinkled with a few discernable spices adjacent to a pile of crackers. Jim picked up a cracker, then using a butter knife, smeared some of the burger on the cracker before sliding it into his mouth.

"What's that?" I asked.

"Cannibal sandwich," he said while chewing.

Huh. I decided I needed to try one. One was all it took. Cannibal sandwiches were never going to be a thing with me.

Jim struck up conversations with people he knew from other retriever trials. And then they began to announce the results. First, the officials ran through the winners for the Derby entries for the young dogs in the competition, honorable mentions, and fourth through first place.

Then it was time for the Amateur class to be announced. They named off three "honorable mentions," but Stoney wasn't among them. Jim's shoulders slumped in disappointment.

"I was hoping for an honorable mention," he said with a sigh. "I thought Stoney did well enough compared to the others."

I guess my screw-ups had cost Jim and Stoney, from my getting too close to the water retrieve and Stoney seeing me, and then maybe somehow Stoney had seen what was going on with the blind placement, despite my best efforts, and oh … crap. I kicked myself. I should have held back. I didn't need to see anything. Crap.

Fourth place.

Third place.

Second place.

First place. "Stone Castle's Yellow Jacket." The announcement hardly made sense. What?! Stoney won?! He did! He took first place! Between Jim and me, I don't know who was happier, but I do know who was more relieved.

Revelation

ONE AFTERNOON IN THE SUMMER OF 1969, I returned home from an afternoon working for Jim Anderson. When I walked into the kitchen of our house, I immediately knew that something was very wrong. On the kitchen table was an arrangement of dishes, including a margarine tub, sugar bowl, salt and pepper shakers, ketchup bottle, and other items. They had been arranged to form a circle. On the plastic lid of the butter tub were scribblings in Magic Marker™, symbols the likes of which I had never seen before.

I didn't understand what that arrangement or the odd symbols meant. Then, at age seventeen, I was confronted by a terrible truth. My mother was mentally ill. I couldn't ignore it any longer.

A few weeks earlier, Mom had left Dad, left our home, and was living with my grandmother in Flower Bay. While the rest of the family was out of our house, she had visited and left a message, that to me, was terrifying in its undecipherability.

Mom began college two years before I did. In 1968, at the age of thirty-three, she enrolled at Lake Superior State College in Sault Ste. Marie, thirty-five miles north of us. She carpooled

to school with several other middle-aged women from the Les
Cheneaux that year.

Her attending college didn't come as a shock to me. Mom
was well-read. Every Sunday, she drove downtown to Arnie's
Mart to buy both the *Detroit Free Press* and the *Detroit News*. I like
that because each paper had different Sunday funnies, but she
liked to compare and contrast the editorials from those newspapers. We subscribed to *The Saturday Evening Post, Look, US News
and World Report, Time,* and *Reader's Digest.* She was interested in
politics and philosophy, as well as her Native American heritage
that she'd just begun exploring.

There was more to it than that. She had skipped a full
grade shortly after World War II and graduated from high
school at the age of seventeen in 1951. She was deeply in love
with a strong, handsome young draftee. At the age of sixteen,
she had driven halfway across the country by herself to see him
inducted into the army. Three months after graduation from
high school, she married my father. Four months after that, I
was born. Shortly thereafter, Dad was ordered to Germany.

Mom claimed that the two of us "grew up together," only
seventeen years apart. Circumstances had robbed her of her late
teens, and college wasn't possible. She escaped her less-than-
happy childhood home and exchanged it for the life of a teenaged stay-at-home mother.

On the other hand, her mother had a teaching degree.
After divorcing my grandfather in the early 1960s, Grandmother
Ione Steel went back to school and earned a Master's Degree in
Education. She supported herself by teaching and by working at
Doc DeLoof's office down by the lakeshore in Cedarville.

I believe Mom felt like she was in competition with my

grandmother, thus the decision to attend college in 1968. She loved it.

She often shared her classroom experiences with us while we ate dinner. Sometimes it was about discussions she had with faculty (who were often young than she). At other times she told a funny story about one of the kids with whom she attended class.

On one occasion, she related a story one of her older classmates had passed along. His mother had attended a Johnny Cash concert in Sault, Ontario, in the early 1950s. Sam said her mother returned from that concert shaking her head. "That kid is never going to make it," she told Sam. Mom and Dad had attended that same concert and were fans of Johnny Cash well before he "made it."

She shared her thoughts on the administration cracking down on an organization trying to gain a foothold among the students, the Students for a Democratic Society, the SDS. She was angered when the college confiscated all the SDS literature on campus. According to Mom, the SDS worked to end the war in Vietnam, to ensure that Americans were free to petition their government, and to eliminate hunger in America. In 1968, those concepts were seditious.

There was one class in particular that caught her attention. The instructor, Dr. Gerald Ringer, challenged his students and their world views. He implied that human destiny was guided in accordance with astrological principles.

Mom had always loved speculation of life beyond this realm and hints of knowledge beyond our ken. She frequently brought home books on those topics, books about Edgar Cayce, a clairvoyant nick-named America's Sleeping Prophet, and Jeane

Dixon, a self-proclaimed psychic and astrologer. In Dr. Ringer, she found someone who could converse fluently in those concepts.

Mom buried herself in classwork, especially the work she was doing in Dr. Ringer's class. She was studying the book of *Revelation*. Her notes began to fill lined yellow legal pads, the pages brimming with her tightly-scripted cursive. The pages of those notebooks curled from the pressure of her BIC™ pen. Page after page was flipped over the top and pinned behind. I read some of her notes and found them to be primarily quotes lifted word-for-word from the Book of Revelation. I couldn't tell if she thought the Apocalypse was coming or if she thought Revelation was a description of the struggle between good and evil.

After Christmas that winter and shortly after I'd turned seventeen, Mom took me to Sault Ste Marie one evening. Dr. Ringer and his wife were hosting a party at his small home on a quiet street near the campus. Guests sat in the Ringer's living room, filling the old sofa and two overstuffed chairs. Lacy ivory curtains hung over the windows. Several of his students seated themselves on the red braided rug that covered most of the floor. I sat cross-legged on the floor at Mom's feet. As the oldest student there, Mom was granted one of the soft chairs by her fellow students. Dr. Ringer pulled a dining room chair into the living room, seated himself, and began.

"We are on the cusp of a new age," he said. "The equinox is about to align with the constellation Aquarius, and a new age of human development will begin. In this new age, humanity," he emphasized, "will finally take control of its own destiny."

Mom squeezed my shoulder and leaned forward to whisper in my ear. I could hear her smiling. "Listen to this," she told me.

"This new age," Ringer continued, "is going to be one of revelation of truth and the advancement of consciousness." The audience looked on, taking in every word, every maxim. Nobody talked like this in Cedarville.

"There will be those whose mental capabilities are enhanced in this new age. They will be able to see the truth. And they will be recognized as the leaders," he added

A brief discussion followed that was mostly Ringer's students asking questions. Shortly thereafter, a dark-haired student in sweater and glasses said he had heard that Dr. Ringer had received a set of drums for Christmas.

Dr. Ringer admitted to that fact and added that he had been practicing.

"Oh, can we hear something?" the student exclaimed.

In a small study off the dining room, there was a set of drums, the likes of which you would see Ringo Starr playing during a Beatles' set. Dr. Ringer queued up The Doors' most recent LP release, *Strange Days*, and "People Are Strange" boomed out of the speakers.

He began tapping the snare drums lightly in time to the music. Once he had the rhythm right, he began using his drumsticks in earnest, pounding out a beat, hitting the cymbals every so often for effect. His focus was intense, his lips pursed, his eyes staring in one direction only. He was in his world.

I was seventeen. I didn't know drugs. But Dr. Ringer's intense focus on his drumming, his immersion in that moment, and his vacant stare while performing had left me uneasy.

After the drumming, the crowd reassembled in the living room. There was more discussion. The night wore on.

"Mom, it's getting late," I said when I got her attention.

"You're right," she said. She pulled the car keys out of her pocket and handed them to me. "You head home. I'm going to stay."

Dad was angry the next morning. He wasn't angry at me.

I told him what had happened. I told him about Ringer's drumming. "It was like he was on drugs," I added.

"Most drummers *are* on drugs," he said, disparaging every rock and roll band I'd ever heard.

Mom returned later that day. I never heard any angry words between them, but I knew that a trust had been breached.

Mom's studies continued into the spring. Her note-taking and transcription of the book of *Revelation* increased.

Spring morphed into summer, and both college and high school academic years ended. I was between my junior and senior years of high school and contemplating summer work opportunities. Those included continuing my part-time work for Jim Anderson, working part-time at Dee's Standard gas station as a pump attendant, or working full-time for the Les Cheneaux Club.

Mom had encouraged me not to go to work full time.

"It's the last summer you will have to be free," she told me. "You'll need to work every summer after you graduate high school to pay for college."

"Did your mother talk to you?" Dad asked one day as I was sitting in our living room reading.

"Yeah, she did," I told Dad, thinking he was referring to my summer work dilemma. I had still not made up my mind. Dad didn't continue with the conversation but rather, turned away and walked back out to the garage.

But, no, Mom had not talked to me.

Later that day, Terrie and I sat in our living room, in the same home that Dad had grown up in, the home where my grandmother had taught us how to drink coffee, in the same room where I learned to roll cigarettes using Bugle Boy papers and tobacco and a rolling machine, while she observed and offered advice from her wicker rocker.

Mom stood in the doorway between the living room and the kitchen and spoke to us.

"I'm leaving your father," Mom said.

Terrie and I sat overwhelmed. The silence was oppressive.

"I guess I'm not surprised," I finally said. To me, their differences had always been obvious.

Mom left to live with her mother, at least for the short term, in Flower Bay. Terrie followed Mom. She was determined to show no favoritism. Her plan was to spend two weeks with Mom followed by two weeks with Dad, alternating until some point in the future when they would both come to their senses.

Over the next several days, Dad and I worked on cooking for ourselves. Neither of us was a good cook, but we could fry meat and potatoes and heat cans of vegetables.

"I love your mother," Dad said. "I even said I would do half the housework if she would come back," he added. I nodded, but I knew it wasn't about housework. With nothing to add, I sat mute.

One night at the dinner table, as we sliced into our fried pork chops amidst heaps of onions and fried potatoes, Dad said to me, "I'm surprised you didn't go to live with your mother."

I looked him in the eye. "Dad, this is my home," I said, allowing just a hint of defiance in my answer.

I believed Dad needed my support more than Mom

needed me. Yes, growing up, it was apparent to me that Terrie was Dad's girl, and I was Mom's boy. But I also thought there was a right and a wrong here. I chose Dad's side.

Our whole family was worried about Mom's behavior. Both grandparents on Mom's side of the family were deeply concerned. There was talk of a "nervous breakdown" on Mom's part. I had no idea what that meant other than that it was something that was to be hidden away, never to be discussed outside the immediate family.

When Dad removed all the guns from the house, I understood that this was serious.

On the day I had returned home from work to find a message from her hidden in the arrangement on the kitchen table, I began to realize the depths into which Mom had plummeted. I tried to hide everything. I hurriedly cleared the table and put things back where they belonged, back to the way they were before. The butter dish went back in the refrigerator . There was nothing I could do about the Magic Marker designs.

When Terrie came home, she saw the butter dish in the refrigerator. "Mom was here, wasn't she?" she said worriedly. I could only nod. There was nothing to verbalize, nothing more talk might make right.

There is no mental illness described as a nervous breakdown. I have only my guess as to what had happened. I think Mom got caught in a tight spot from which no obvious exit existed. As the pressure increased, she became incapable of resisting her need to escape. Eventually, it broke her ability to determine what was real and what was not.

At the urging of both her parents, she saw a psychiatrist regularly. Dad kept Terrie and me apprised as much as possible, with what he could share from the psychiatrist.

"Her doctor says she is really smart," he once offered. "Your mom asks a question, and then later she circles around to ask the same question a different way."

In late summer, Mom returned home. By the end of the summer, things had almost returned to normal. On the outside, she was as cheerful as ever. Whatever burden she had borne that caused her nervous breakdown was no longer apparent.

I began my senior year at high school. On the first day back in September, our principal, John Duncan, pulled me aside as I walked down the brown-tiled hallway between classes.

"I was sorry to hear about your Mom's nervous breakdown this summer," he said. "The same thing happened in our family. I know how hard it was for you, but it will all work out."

I didn't say "thank you." I just nodded my head. I didn't say anything. But now, I realized that people outside our immediate family knew. It was no longer hidden away, a realization that made me ashamed.

For the next six years, the four of us lived our lives in our old house across the road from the Spring Lodge. We pretended there was no problem.

I graduated from high school in 1970. Terrie followed in 1972, and then she got married.

I was graduated from Lake Superior State College with a Bachelor of Science in Biology in 1974. I lived at "home" in the winter of '74-'75. That spring, I left home for good, moving to Cadillac, where I accepted a permanent job with the U.S. Forest Service. Kathryn and I had agreed upon a date to get married.

I received a letter from Mom that fall. It was hand-written with ballpoint pen, in her tightly controlled cursive on lined, yellow legal pad paper.

"Dear Pete," she wrote, "I am alive and well and living in St. Ignace...."

Mom had left Dad for the second and final time. This time, however, she had maintained her sanity.

Little St. Martin's Reef

JIM ANDERSON HAD WHAT HE CALLED A HEART CONDITION, so it wasn't smart for him to hunt on his own. He needed someone to wrestle bags of decoys in and out of the boat and to load and unload the canoe off the top of his old green station wagon. Jim needed a hunting partner to handle the heavy lifting. I was available and became his duck hunting protege. In his shirt pocket, Jim carried pills that I might need to administer to him if he had a heart problem while hunting. Luckily, that situation never came to pass.

One Friday in late October 1973, Jim called me at home with a change to our Saturday duck hunting plan.

"The wind is going to be just right for hunting the reef off Little St. Martin's Island," he said. "We need to get an early start. Why don't you come by around 5:00 am? I'll have breakfast ready, so we can get to the reef before shooting hours."

Okay. I was there the next morning in the dark, a gentle northwest wind rustling the dead leaves of the balsam poplars, known locally as bam. The cool, damp air carried the scent of dead leaves and the promise of a chilly boat ride. St. Martin's Island Reef was out on the Big Lake, about five miles outside the protected waters of the islands.

Jim had made pancakes, and though he wasn't supposed to eat any, there was a plate of bacon, too. Jim turned on his weather radio to check on forecast updates since Friday night. No, the forecast hadn't changed: winds of ten to fifteen knots out of the northwest all day were still predicted, as were mostly cloudy conditions with no precipitation and a daytime high temperature in the low forties.

After breakfast, we made our way down to the boathouse in the dark. The Boston Whaler was tucked inside out of the weather. Jim pointed out sacks of Italian decoys for me to place in the Whaler. The plastic decoys were realistic and hollow, which made them a heck of a lot better looking than the cedar decoys my friends and I carved with hatchets and wood rasps. Plus, they were made in Italy! They were a whole lot lighter, too! I loaded several dozen bluebill, redhead, and bufflehead decoys into the Whaler. I stacked the cased shotguns in a safe spot and made sure our shell bags were in the boat too. My little duffel bag held a box of number six shot, two and three-quarters-inch, twelve-gauge shells, three peanut butter sandwiches, and a quart of hot tea in my stainless-steel Uno Vac™ vacuum bottle.

Jim double-checked fuel levels in the red six-gallon gas tanks before starting the engine. While it warmed up, I untied the boat. We backed out of the lighted boathouse into the dark morning, turned into the wind, and headed northwest up the Snows Channel into the breeze. There was just enough light to make out where we were in the narrow channel at any given time. We zipped past the Club Dock at the golf course, past the Club Dock on the Marquette Island side, around the Club Point, and into Hessel Bay.

The ride wasn't uncomfortable. There was a small

windshield in front of the bench where Jim sat at the controls. I huddled next to him, my head down. I didn't need to see where we were going. That was Jim's job.

Just south of Hessel, we turned southwest. The light breeze kicked the spray back along the boat, not enough to get us too wet, but I was glad Jim was catching most of it. On we went, out of Hessel Bay, past Brown's Point, through Wilderness Bay, and then past Long Island and Birch Island. We cut through the waves to the West Entrance to the Les Cheneaux Islands, then past Point Brule, and onto the Big Lake.

Jim leaned over to me and yelled over the whine of the sixty-horse Johnson outboard, "Now we head straight for the lights on the Mackinac Bridge for five miles and then turn right." Five miles? I'd never been out on the Big Lake that far before.

"In 1972, this reef is where I found what might have been the last cormorant nest on the Great Lakes," Jim yelled above the whine of the outboard.

Cormorants? On the Great Lakes? I'd never seen one.

"DDT nearly eliminated them from the Great Lakes, just like bald eagles. There was one juvenile bird near the nest that looked like it had died about halfway to the water. It was a really sad scene."

We arrived at the reef, actually a low, rocky island, an hour before legal shooting hours began. The reef was about 500 feet long east-to-west and 50 to 200 feet wide, most of its length less than three feet higher than the lake.

The water levels of the Great Lakes fluctuate from year to year. During the current low-water year, this little reef was exposed as an island. During periods of high water, the "island" was inundated. Most of the rocks were bowling-ball sized, well-rounded from grinding under glaciers thousands of years ago, the several glaciations that had carved the Great Lakes. Tufts of willow brush sprouted here and there.

We carefully placed the Italian decoys, grouping them by species, about thirty-five yards off the east end of the island, the downwind end. When my friends and I hunted ducks over decoys, our decoy placement technique was far more haphazard. It often required adjustment after the sun came up when we could see decoys bumping together with crossed lines and decoys that had landed upside down. Jim, on the other hand, was always determined to get it right the first time.

With the decoys in place, Jim ran the Whaler upwind to a small cove of protected shallow water on the northwest end. Jim pulled into it. He shut down the motor and set the anchor. Pulling up our hip boots, we waded ashore with our shotguns, stools, and shell bags.

We picked our way across the cobble, taking care not to turn an ankle until we reached the east end of the reef. Two clumps of willow were to be the basis of our duck blind. I scouted around that end of the reef and hauled back dead willow branches and driftwood that we added to the blind until we felt comfortable that ducks would have a difficult time seeing us as they approached our decoy set from downwind.

While waiting for shooting hours (thirty minutes before legal sunrise), I pulled a peanut butter and jelly sandwich from my pack and poured myself a cup of hot tea to counteract the chill from our long boat ride.

When shooting hours arrived, I put away my thermos and food. I loaded my shotgun. Then we watched. We scanned the sky in front of us though we would each look over our shoulders every few minutes to watch for ducks coming at us from upwind. Duck hunting, for me, always meant chafed skin around my collar and sore neck muscles.

There weren't very many ducks flying, though a small flock of bluebills buzzed over the decoys at one point during the morning. Jim shot twice and killed one. I emptied my pump shotgun at the flock to no avail. My last shot was at ducks that had already swung out of range. In those days, I was a poor "wing" shot. When I hunted with friends, we would often wait for the ducks to land in the decoys before shooting. Jim was aghast when I told him that. To him, shooting ducks on the water was not sporting. To me, shooting ducks on the water meant not wasting shells.

Around mid-morning, the wind came up a little with occasional gusts that swirled the dead yellow willow leaves littering the rocky shore. We thought that might get some birds to move around, and sure enough, a flock of a dozen ducks startled us when they flew over us from behind. To our surprise, they circled about a hundred yards down wind and came back toward the decoys. We crouched in anticipation, thumbs on the guns' safeties, waiting for that moment when they came within range, when we would jump to our feet and shoot. They flared as though they had seen something they didn't like in our decoys or the blind. They circled again at sixty yards, just outside the decoys, still out of range.

Eventually, the ducks landed on the water about seventy-five yards from our blind, well out of range. Then they began swimming in toward our set of decoys. At fifty yards out, the extreme limits of the range of our shotguns, the ducks swam back out. Then they swam in again. And again, they turned away.

"Something is scaring those birds," Jim declared. "They wanted to come into the decoys." We checked our blind for gaps in the brush. I laid my stainless-steel thermos on its side and pulled some grass over it.

Jim watched the flock through binoculars. "They're not mallards," he said. "They're not widgeons, not teal."

They swam in closer. At fifty yards, they turned away again. "I think those are gadwalls!" he exclaimed. I'd never seen gadwalls. They weren't common ducks in our neck of the woods. We watched them intensely.

Jim was exasperated. We checked the blind again. Nothing obvious stuck out as unnatural that might cause ducks to flare. I looked over my right shoulder. The Whaler was bobbing in the waves, headed downwind, a hundred feet offshore. The higher wind gusts had caused it to pull anchor and float out of its little cove! "Jim! The boat!"

"Oh, no!" he said. "You're going to have to go get it, Pete. You might have to get wet."

He was right. If the Whaler didn't get hung up on Goose Island nearly seven miles downwind, the next stop was the Bruce Peninsula in Ontario, about 200 miles to the southeast.

Not thinking, I laid my shotgun down, and jumped up. I ran to the water's edge and then sloshed into the lake. The rocks were round and algae-covered, making for unsure footing. Soon I was in knee-deep. Then I stepped off a ledge and I was thigh deep. One more step and my hip boots filled with the Big Lake's icy water. I could barely make any progress trying to swing one foot in front of the other in those boots. With another step the chilly water was crotch deep and then waist deep. The boat gently rocked, still more than twenty-five feet away.

When I got chest deep, I tried to jump to avoid being swept over by a swell from behind. With my feet no longer in contact with the bottom, I began frantically dog-paddling with my hands while struggling to kick with my water-filled hip boots. I moved barely faster than the boat was drifting. I slowly gained on it; fifteen feet; ten feet; five feet; and I was there!

I grabbed a gunwale a foot-and-a-half above the water line with one hand and then the other. I tried to hoist myself aboard. I was only able to get one elbow over the gunwale. I didn't have the strength to pull my waterlogged self and my hip boots full of water on board. I hung on the gunwale, exhausted from my swim, bobbing downwind with the boat.

With my left hand, I unsnapped my left hip boot from my belt and peeled it down my thigh. Using my right foot, I was able to push my left boot off my foot. I grabbed it, dumped the water out of it, and heaved it into the Whaler. Hanging from the gunwale, I repeated that with my right boot and tossed it into the Whaler as well. I removed my water-soaked hunting jacket and flung it into the boat.

Thus lightened, I finally dragged myself further up the side of the boat, catching the lip of the gunwale with my rib cage. Then I hoisted my left leg over the gunwale and rolled into the boat. I was shivering, both from the cold and the exhaustion.

Okay. Key in the ignition. I squeezed the fuel bulb several times until it was firm, indicating that the fuel system was primed. The motor tilted down, so the prop was in the water. I turned the key. The engine turned over rapidly for five seconds, but it did not fire.

Again. This time, I turned the ignition for ten seconds. Still no fire.

I looked back at Jim, now a hundred yards upwind, still standing in the blind. I gave him the universal signal for "I don't know what's wrong," shaking my head from side to side accompanied by an exaggerated shoulder shrug with arms bent out to the side, palms up.

Jim was giving me hand signals. Pointing. Pushing. Pulling. And shouting. I could barely hear him over the wind and the slosh of waves against the side of the boat.

What was he saying? "Boat?" Why would he say "boat"? I looked around to see if there was another boat near us. No. We were alone.

Then he put both hands around his neck. No, no... It was "CHOKE!" Choke! There was an un-labeled chrome knob on the dash. Was that the choke? I pulled it out and cranked the engine again. The engine fired! I gradually eased the choke back in, and the motor began running smoothly. Dragging myself up to the bow, I hauled in the anchor that was hanging straight down, nowhere near the lake bottom. Back on the bench behind the windshield, I put the engine in gear.

I slowly motored back toward the reef, and Jim caught the bow of the Whaler before I beached it on the rocks. He tossed the anchor line onto the beach and made several trips between the boat and the blind, twenty-five feet away. He emptied the shotguns and slid them into the leather gun cases. He retrieved the stools and the shell bags, loading them all into the boat.

Then we picked up the decoys in a growing chill breeze cutting in from the northwest. One at a time, we grabbed each decoy as we passed through the decoy spread; grabbed them by the head as we slipped past, holding the decoy with the left hand while wrapping the line in a figure-eight pattern, around the tail, around the neck, back around the tail, and finally wrapping the ling, thin lead strap anchor around the decoy's neck to secure it. Then we tossed them into mesh bags by species.

It must have taken us forty-five minutes to pick up the decoys. By then, I'd been soaked and exposed to the wind for nearly an hour. It was time to get me home.

The breeze had stiffened. We quartered into the waves. The bow of the Whaler climbed each wave, hesitated, then pounded onto the next wave, shooting an arc of spray into the wind, which quickly hurled the icy water drops back over the boat. I was worried.

Jim sensed that. "These boats will take a lot more sea than people are comfortable with," he shouted over the wind. "You just have to 'play' each wave as it comes." Jim had one hand on the wheel and his other on the throttle as he adjusted the boat's speed and orientation to each wave.

In thirty minutes, we were back within the lee of Point Brule and no longer exposed to the pounding waves of the big lake. We picked up speed. I huddled as much as I could behind the small wind screen of the Whaler.

Halfway across Hessel Bay we noticed a fourteen-foot StarCraft jammed with four people dressed in camouflage. As we approached, they stood and waved their arms. Jim slowed and pulled up near the old aluminum boat that had about half its paint flaked away.

"Our motor quit," said the gray-haired, heavy-set man at the tiller, next to a silent fifteen-horsepower Johnson outboard that looked older than my dad. "Can you run us into the marina?"

Jim looked at me. I shrugged. We couldn't leave those guys. They didn't even have a paddle. And the wind would have taken them another two to three miles downwind into the back of the bay.

"We'll give you a tow," Jim said, "but it's going to be a pretty fast tow. I've got to get this guy," gesturing at me sitting there soaked, "back home where he can get some dry clothes on."

They tossed Jim a ratty old bow line. He looked at it and shrugged before looping it around a cleat at the corner of the transom. He made sure the line was clear of the prop, started the engine, put it in gear, and slowly tightened the line between the two.

"Hang on," he told the passengers in the little aluminum boat before he eased the throttle forward. When he saw the towed boat riding safely behind us, Jim increased the speed. Those guys in the other boat were catching a steady spray, but Jim made no effort to slow down. "They might get a little wet," he said with a grin.

In a few minutes, we were inside the government breakwater of Hessel harbor. Jim swung the Whaler around, gently depositing the towed boat up against the dock. He untied their bowline, and without a backward glance, we were off again, at full speed, down the length of Hessel Bay, round Club Point, past the golf course, and back inside Jim's boathouse.

I put on my hip boots, gathered my gear, trudged down the dock, then up the path past the Anderson house, up the driveway, and down the street a hundred yards to my home.

There it was time to dry off, drink some hot tea, and dress in dry clothes.

A couple of years later, Ralph told me that when his dad had heard the story, he had gotten angry with Jim and let him know it. Bruce knew how dangerous the big lake was, especially in the fall. Jim hadn't been thinking when asked me to retrieve the boat.

The worst thing that would have happened if we had let the boat go is that we would have spent a cold day and maybe even a night on the reef before being found. That would have been easier to stomach than the possibility of someone losing his life swimming after a boat being blown downwind.

I never thought much about that day other than the fact I got soaked out on the big lake in October. I was just grateful that I had seen the last of that Little St. Martin's Island reef.

Or so I'd thought.

A Real Outdoor Writer

ONE SUMMER, JIM INTRODUCED ME to one of his Cincinnati friends, Karl Maslowski. He was in his late fifties with a well-trimmed white mustache. His silvery hair was receding along his temples, framing piercing gray/blue eyes. He smiled as we shook hands. He was a friendly guy.

Karl was an outdoor columnist for the *Cincinnati Enquirer* and a wildlife photographer. I learned that he had filmed many of the scenes for *Beaver Valley*, a nature short I had seen on the Disneyland television series. I was impressed!

One foggy morning, Jim asked me to take Karl brook trout fishing, as Karl hadn't fished any of the local creeks. I agreed and ran back home to get my spinning rod sporting a brand-new Mitchell 308 spinning reel (which was a step up from my old plastic Zebco reel), and a canvas/mesh creel with a shoulder strap.

It turned out that Karl was interested in more than just fishing. He asked questions about what kinds of wildlife might be present in the area. He said the habitat we were in reminded him of places where cottontail rabbits would be found along the Ohio River.

"No cottontails," I said. "We've only got snowshoe hares around here."

He asked about deer hunting and what caliber rifle I used.

"I started hunting with buckshot in Dad's old Fox double-barrel, but I graduated to a Winchester .308," I said.

"What weight bullet?" he asked.

"180 grain."

"That seems like far more bullet than you need for white-tailed deer," he commented skeptically.

"We hunt in heavy brush areas," I said. "Lighter bullets deflect too much." I didn't really know, but I'd heard Dad and his friends talking about that at deer camp.

I told Karl I liked to hunt ducks and owned a copy of the *Duck Hunter's Bible* by Erwin A. Bauer. "Oh, I know Joe," Karl said.

"Joe?" I asked.

"He goes by Joe," Karl said. I mentioned other outdoor writers whose work I devoured in monthly issues of *Field & Stream, Outdoor Life,* and *Sports Afield.* Karl knew them all. Was I impressed? Oh, yes.

I could only imagine a life spent hunting, fishing, and writing about it in national magazines. Not that I was ever going to do that. My focus was on earning enough money to go to college, study wildlife and fisheries, and hope to get a job as a biologist. Writing about hunting and fishing in exotic places? Not likely.

We drove down a two-track road near the upper stretches of a small creek. While the creek itself wasn't much for fishing, two beaver ponds held some nice fish. With some effort, we could entice a couple of trout to bite our small spinners tipped with garden worms.

We pulled the car off the two-track road and parked. We grabbed our fishing rods out of the trunk and made sure we had extra hooks and sinkers in case we got snagged and had to replace fishing tackle. We eased down an almost hidden path through the forest of paper birch and balsam fir, past fallen aspens with rotten trunks ripped open, blown over in a recent high wind. When we passed a patch of bracken ferns, I stopped to break off several fronds to place in my creel.

Then we broke out of the woods and descended a short slope down to a beaver pond with a low layer of mist still hanging over it.

A kingfisher rattled its call as it pitched and swooped across to the other side of the beaver dam. This was an old pond. Many of the trees that had been flooded when the pond was first constructed by beavers and were long dead, having fallen over. The few remaining dead trees were smooth and gray as their bark had finally sloughed off.

We walked past this pond. Better fishing was to be had at a pond created when another family of beavers had constructed a new dam downstream. Newer ponds were more productive for brook trout, it seemed.

Karl and I skirted the flooded timber around the new pond until we arrived at the new dam. We edged our way out along a very narrow path of beaver-chewed limbs and mud that comprised the dam. Karl prepared to cast his fishing line from the dam into the open water.

"The best way to fish beaver ponds," I said, "is to wade around the edges of the dam and try to get your bait into the original stream channel where it's deeper." Karl worked his way down the beaver dam to where the water was flowing down-stream. The deepest water was in front of him.

I walked back the way we came and eventually steeled myself into wading into the cold water in my tennis shoes and blue jeans. I waded through the knee-deep water, working my way through the standing timber until I saw brush that had once defined the edge of the original stream bank. A hairy wood-pecker flew onto a dead aspen and began tapping on the trunk for insects buried within the tree's decaying heart.

From there, I began to flip my bait underhanded into what I was pretty sure was the original stream channel. The bait would slowly sink to the bottom before I began a slow retrieve. I continued to cast with varying degrees of accuracy until one of my casts ended up flying over a dead aspen branch. Jerking my line back only had the effect of my bait quickly wrapping around the branch three or four times. That was a "snag" there was no way out of.

I pulled on the monofilament line until it broke. Reeling in the slack line, I tied a single-bladed spinner on with an improved clinch knot and added a lead split shot six inches from the hook, crimping it onto the line with my teeth. I slid a small earthworm over the thin wire hook. Moving further up the creek through the flooded trees, I cast my bait ahead, careful to avoid entangling my line again.

The morning sun burned off the last of the mist. I edged out closer to deep water, slowly shuffling my tennis shoe-clad feet, taking care not to step into deep holes. Ahead of me, I could make out a disturbance in the shallow water, a puff of mud where a fish had hidden before darting off in a hurry. Opening the bail of my Mitchell 308, I held the line in the crook of my index finger. I flipped the bait out ahead of me and—at the right moment—straightened my finger, pointing at the place I hoped my bait might land. Close enough, I let the bait sink. Then the belly of the line tightened, and the rod tip twitched! I set the hook and reeled in a wiggling little eight-inch brook trout!

"Got one!" I hollered in Karl's direction.

I quickly killed it by bending its head back, breaking its neck, and tucked it into my fern-lined creel. Scooping up water in my hand, I ladled it into the creel to help keep the fish cool.

Wading further, I caught another brook trout, a nine-incher. This was almost bragging-sized. Around here, a ten-inch trout was one that people would admire. We ended our fishing trip around noon when we joined up and headed back to the car. I gave Karl the trout I'd caught, as he was hoping to cook up a trout breakfast the next day for his wife, Edna, and the Andersons.

A couple of months after the brook trout fishing trip, Jim gave me a clipping from the *Cincinnati Enquirer*. It was Karl's weekly column, "Naturalist Afield." In it, he described fishing for brook trout in a remote beaver pond with his local guide, Pete Griffin. I was thrilled. Outside the occasional Honor Roll mention in our local paper, *The Weekly Wave*, I'd never seen my name in print. And it wasn't just any print, it was in an outdoor column by a real outdoor writer in a big-city newspaper!

I went fishing for smallmouth bass with Karl. The first smallmouth Karl hooked put up a great fight and jumped clear out of the water, throwing spray that caught the late afternoon sun. When he brought it to the boat, Karl lifted it out of the water by its lower jaw, gently removed the hook, and slipped it back into the water.

"I've never seen a fish jump like that before," I exclaimed. I could hardly wait to catch one myself.

"Oh, the good ones will often do that," he said smiling.

At the end of that first fishing trip for bass, Karl gave me several lures from his tackle box: Pikey-Minnow™, Jitterbug™, Hula Popper™, and River Runts™. I still have those lures nearly fifty years later. Over the next couple of years, we fished places I'd never thought to fish in the Les Cheneaux Islands; a gravelly point at the entrance to Peck Bay, Middle Entrance Reef, and other submerged shoals.

The last time I saw Karl was the mid-1970s, when I'd driven Jeanne Anderson from Upper Michigan back to the Andersons' home in Cincinnati. Jim was staying on longer in the Les Cheneaux to hunt ducks.

The Andersons had arranged for me to fly back home, but I had a day or so before that flight. Jim told Jeanne to give me access to his den and left instructions "not to disturb him while he's in there." That evening I looked through Jim's library of hunting and fishing books. I perused his photo album of him and his brother fishing for lake trout on Lake Superior in the 1930s. The boat was wooden, the fishing rods stout with large reels filled with wire lines. He and his brothers held up dozens of big lake trout. I could only imagine. His grand memories were all before the lamprey eel scourge devastated the trout population.

Best of all, Jim had arranged for me to spend half a day with Karl in Cincinnati, looking at some of the habitats along the Ohio River, identifying tree species that I'd never seen before, and looking for wildlife. On the way out of one of the nature centers, Karl braked the car to a quick halt, pointing out the driver's side window at a tree.

"There's a red-phase screech owl!" he exclaimed.

Sure enough, sitting inside the rotted scar of a branch that had pulled off the tree long ago sat a small owl with rusty red feathers, staring back at us. That Karl had seen the small bird as he was driving amazed me.

He showed me Osage oranges that lined some of the streets, their spiky orange fruits littering the roadways.

He pointed out persimmons. They were falling from the trees at that time of the fall. He encouraged me to eat one. Out of curiosity, I picked one up off the grass and checked for dirt and worms before cautiously taking a bite of it. It was so sweet! "People sometimes spread raw, very ripe persimmons on their toast like jelly in the morning," he said.

I hung out while Karl attended to business in his home office. I gazed at letters thumbtacked to his bulletin board, at the awards he had earned hanging on the wall. There was a photo of Karl's, a gray squirrel hanging upside down from a branch, holding on with one leg, the cover of a national wildlife magazine. Some wit had pasted a hand-written cartoonish voice-bubble caption above the squirrel: "Take the picture already, Karl, this nail in my foot is killing me!"

Over the years, I watched for Karl's name in my outdoor magazines, pleased when I saw him mentioned in an article about fishing for Arctic char in the Northwest Territories. I saw his screen credits at the end of wildlife documentaries. I always smiled. If I was around my folks, I would point it out.

"I took Karl Maslowski fishing for brook trout that one time," I'd remind them.

To me, he was a great guy, doing just the kinds of stuff I wanted to do for the rest of my life, except that Karl was doing it for a living. I could only hope at some point in my future that I could manage those hunting and fishing trips after work, on weekends, or during limited vacations.

Karl, however, had made a career of being in the woods, taking photographs and writing articles for newspapers and magazines. That hardly seemed like work at all. Now, I had a focus worthy of my aspirations.

Today, when I take stock of my life, of where I've been and what I've done, I come to realize that I have lived much of what I had aspired to. I live in Alaska, where I hunt and fish in varied and remote locations. I've caught grayling and Arctic char. I've hunted Dall sheep and caribou above the Arctic Circle. I've seen and photographed whales and Alaska brown bears. I have shared my photographs, videos, and stories of wild places and sporting adventures with thousands of people every year through library talks and books. My work as a naturalist on cruise ships, including Disney's, has presented an interesting coincidence of careers.

My brief companionship with Karl Maslowski helped enable me to see what was possible even if I did not realize it at the time. It wasn't until much later in life that I would understand just how much of a difference Karl Maslowski made, but not just in my life. He revolutionized wildlife photography and filming in the country long before he volunteered for the army and served as a combat photographer in World War II. He returned from the war to lead the effort to establish a park system and natural history centers in Cincinnati.

Karl's family has carried on the family business of wildlife photography and videography. I recently corresponded with Karl's son about our shared memories of the Andersons and some of the places we both knew in the Eastern Upper Peninsula. I was pleased to donate to an effort to produce a documentary regarding Karl Maslowski's revolutionary career in wildlife photography, his time as a combat photographer in World War II, and his conservation efforts in the Cincinnati area.

Thanks, Karl.

The Reef Revisited

I was still working for the US Forest Service in Cadillac during the fall of 1975, still driving back home to the U.P. frequently, especially for duck season. Jim Anderson and I continued duck hunting together. Jim had me along as insurance in case anything went wrong, as well for companionship.

One dark morning I walked down the road to the Anderson place, cradling my new Winchester twelve-gauge shotgun in its weather-proof case. My shell bag was slung over my shoulder. It was weighed down with a stainless-steel vacuum bottle of hot tea, a couple of peanut butter and jelly sandwiches, and a box of shotgun shells. The olive drab shell bag with leather strap was formerly a canvas book bag purchased at Lake Superior State College. A number of graduates of LSSC claimed the book bag was the best thing they ever got out of college. Most of them were kidding. Probably.

I entered the Anderson kitchen, where Jim and his guest were finishing up breakfast. Jim introduced me to John, a game warden from Kentucky. John was visiting that weekend specifically to hunt ducks with Jim. He was much younger than Jim, perhaps in his late thirties, with sandy brown hair and a thin face.

There was a problem. Jim wasn't feeling good. He said that he wouldn't be able to go hunting that morning and suggested that John and I go without him.

Jim suggested that I drive the boat to the reef just off Little St. Martin's Island. The weather and the wind were perfect for that location. They had loaded the *Missy* the night before with decoys and a fifteen-foot aluminum canoe.

"Jim, I've only ever been to that reef once," I said, objecting to the idea of running his inboard-outboard in the dark. "I'm not sure I can even find it," I added.

"That's no problem," Jim said. "Once you get out of Hessel, you just set a course for the lights of the Mackinac Bridge. After about five miles, turn right," he said. "You won't have any problem finding it."

"Well, okay," I said with more than a little reluctance.

Jim held the front door open as John and I exited. "Good luck ... and be safe," he admonished.

John and I carried our guns and shell bags down to the green boathouse. We stashed our gear. I started the engine, and John cast off.

In the Snows Channel, we encountered a middling breeze and found just enough light to navigate the dark channel between the darker shorelines of the mainland and Marquette Island. I managed to avoid hitting any of the green or red buoys that marked rocks or shallow water hazards.

Soon enough, we rounded Club Point into Hessel Bay. Another mile or so, we were to Hessel, where I eased the boat to the left, skirting Brown's Point and staying well to the east of Haven and Goat Islands, which were still invisible in the pre-dawn dark. It was like I could sense them laying there just off to starboard. "So far, so good," I thought. I'd been through these waters enough to know them pretty well.

The boat skimmed along the water smoothly, past Long and Birch Islands. Passing the line between Coates Point and Point Brule, we exited West Entrance onto the big lake. There was still very little wind, but we encountered a gentle swell from the southeast, the remnants of a robust weather system that had passed during the night. There was no fog. The lights on the two towers of the Mackinac Bridge shone on the dark horizon. Opened in 1957, the bridge spanned the Straits of Mackinac, dividing Lake Michigan on the west from Lake Huron on the east. I gently guided the boat onto a course directly at those lights.

Our boat rocked from side to side in the swell as we headed southwest toward the bridge.

Ten minutes or so into that heading, I recalled Jim's words: "Just set a course for the lights on the Mackinac Bridge. After about five miles, turn right." I gently spun the chrome wheel and eased the boat into a right turn in the dark.

"We should be coming up on the reef any minute, John. Watch for it," I shouted. The bow of the boat dropped as I eased the throttle handle back to an idle. No low rocky island appeared in the dark before us. Had I gone too far? Not far enough? The boat bobbed in the swell coming at us from astern as we idled onward. We scanned the dark for a sign that we might be near Little St. Martin Island reef but saw nothing ahead.

Crunch! Crunch! The boat shuddered.

Oh, no! Shutting the engine down, I grabbed a flashlight

off the dash of the boat and shone it down into the green water. John and I leaned over the rail. Only a couple of feet underwater were rocks ... Lots of rocks. I had run us onto a reef just off St. Martin's Point, not the reef off Little St. Martin's Island.

The boat was still rolling in the swell, so we weren't entirely grounded. I ran back to the dash and raised the outdrive out of the water.

Two inches of each of the three blades of the propeller had been chewed off. Dammit. I'd hit a rock with the prop, leaving broken and jagged edges. With some care, I slowly lowered the outdrive until the prop was barely under water and restarted the engine. Slowly we backed off the reef into a safer depth.

We soon found we could run the boat at about one-third throttle without the boat vibrating too uncomfortably. After some discussion, we decided to continue to our original destination, just two miles further ahead. By then, the sky was becoming lighter. We could barely make out the rocky island where we would be hunting.

We limped along, eventually reaching the un-named treeless island. Anchoring just off the place where we would set up our duck blind, we pulled the canoe out of the boat and set it alongside. We shrugged into our life jackets. After I climbed into the stern of the canoe, John handed me bags of decoys, our shotguns, stools, and camouflaged cloth to supplement the meager brushy blind. Then he gingerly lowered himself into the bow of the canoe.

We left Lady, Jim's Labrador retriever, in the boat while we set the decoys out. After dropping our gear at the blind, we paddled back out to the big boat and tied up. I fired up the engine and slowly motored several hundred yards away from the blind, far enough away that the big white boat wouldn't scare any ducks into avoiding our setup.

We set the anchor, and I carefully climbed down into the canoe, pitching gently in the swell off the big lake. Gingerly, John joined me in the canoe to paddle to our blind, and our hunting began. Small flocks of ducks flew back and forth in the early dawn light. It promised to be a good day for duck hunting.

Lady balanced on the gunwale of the big boat, looking down into the canoe bobbing about three feet below her.

"C'mon, Lady," John said, encouraging her to jump into the canoe. Lady jumped.

In a moment, my world turned green, cold, and wet.

Have you ever had one of those experiences when, in the blink of an eye, your world changed drastically? The change is so abrupt and so complete, it leaves you wondering what just happened.

I surfaced, sputtering. Lady was near me, dog paddling near the overturned canoe.

"John!" I shouted. "Are you OK?"

"Yeah!" he shouted back. "I'm going to get into the boat," he said.

He swam to the stern of the big boat and—using the outdrive as a ladder—climbed over the stern into the cockpit. John called to Lady, pulling her aboard with some struggle.

Meanwhile, I rolled into the swamped canoe to keep it close to the big boat. On my knees, I paddled, trying to keep the bow pointed into the swells off the big lake. It turned out to be an impossible job. The force of the swells pressured the canoe to turn broadside to the waves. I couldn't even stay inside the canoe as each swell caused the canoe to roll.

John threw me a line from the boat. I tied the line to the canoe, and he pulled me to the boat. I climbed over the stern into the cockpit.

We turned the canoe over, emptying the water out, and hauled it aboard. There was no question as to whether or not we were going to continue hunting, as cold and wet as we were. We pulled anchor and motored over to the decoys, picking them up from the big boat. Neither of us was too eager to get back into the canoe. Luckily, we had put our gear ashore before our disaster. We put the canoe back in the water and retrieved our shotguns, stools, and camouflaged cloth from the shore blind.

We vibrated back home at one-third throttle, hobbled by our damaged prop. "Well," John said, "the only fair thing to do is to buy Jim a new prop, and we'll split the cost."

I had no idea what a new prop might cost, but it was the right thing to do. It was actually more than fair to me, considering John bore no fault for running up on the reef in the dark. That was on me. We arrived back at Jim's boathouse mid-morning. John and I squished up the flagstone path to the house.

John told our story to Jim. I offered my apology. John offered to pay for a new prop.

"No," said Jim, shaking his head, "we'll just chalk that up to experience."

Big Dog

A Princess cruise ship was moored at the Smith Cove Cruise Terminal in Seattle one summer afternoon in 2015. I was on board to give a presentation about living off the land in Alaska on its northbound cruise to the Great Land. The ship pulled away from the peer as the sun began its descent in the west. The angle of the light on the city skyline, including the Space Needle, called for a photo. Using my new "smart phone," I took a picture and immediately posted it to Facebook.

Shortly after posting, an old friend from my hometown posted a comment: "I live in Seattle! You're here? Let's get together!"

Dan had been a year behind me in high school. That class-based society usually meant older students paid no attention to younger students because, well, "What did *they* know?"

Dan's father, Gayle, however, had been a Boy Scout leader for a number of years when I was in the Scouting organization. Gayle, along with Archie Dunn, Cleon Moss, and Roy Dutcher, tended a small Scout troop on adventures on the waters and in the woods of the Les Cheneaux Islands. I hadn't appreciated, when I was younger, just what a difference their volunteering had made in my life. That particular trip on Princess wasn't my last trip through Seattle that year, so Dan and I made plans to meet for dinner at the next opportunity.

When that time came, Dan and his wife Gail picked me up at my hotel and took me out to dinner at a small Mexican restaurant on the south end of town. Over pre-dinner beers, we caught up on what was happening in our lives.

Then Dan and I started sharing memories of growing up in the Les Cheneaux. A memory on the part of one of us led to a memory from the other.

"Yeah, we bought a house on Lakeside Road around 1964," I said.

Then Dan launched into a memory: "I remember a heck of a party on Lakeside Road that ended in a fire lane at the water's edge. It was a real event, dozens of locals and summer kids, kegs of beer.

"When it was time for me to get going home, a guy offered to give me a ride. He looked a bit wild, but it was the '70s. Everybody looked a bit rough.

"Anyways, I climbed into his car, a '67 Camaro.

"We're just getting going when he looks at me and asks, 'Have you ever been in a car wreck?' 'No,' I tell him, wondering what the heck he's got in mind.

"Well, he mashes the gas pedal to the floor, runs straight off the road at the first corner, right into a damned 20-inch maple tree.

"Geez, I hit the dash, my face mashed up against the window. I had blood running into my eyes.

"I look over to see if he's alright. He looks at me and says, 'Well, now you can say you've been in a car wreck.'

"I've still got a scar," Dan said, pointing to a thin white line on his forehead.

"Hokey smokes!" I said. And then I got this weird feeling. "That guy, that wasn't ... the Big Dog, was it?"

Dan looked at me hard. "How the hell did you know that?"

"I've got my own Big Dog story," I replied.

Right around the summer of 1970, my friend Al and I were planning a camping and trout fishing up Cedar Creek. I suggested we get a jug of Mogen David Concord Grape wine, specifically. We were both under-aged. I had not yet developed a taste for either beer or hard liquor, but wine was palatable.

"Oh no," Al said. "Mogen David Blackberry is the best. I know somebody we can get to buy it for us."

That was settled. The guy who knew the buyer had the final say.

Following my friend's directions, I pulled my 1960 Ford Galaxy into a short driveway leading to a tiny house, sided with dingy gray asbestos tiles. Its shingled roof was covered in leaves and pine needles, green moss growing in clumps out of the gutters. In the fading light of the evening, it appeared no bigger than a summer resort cottage with two bedrooms and a combined kitchen/dining area.

"The Big Dog just got back from Vietnam. I think that's why he calls himself that," Al said as though he were warning me. We climbed the stacked concrete block steps to the door, and Al knocked.

A short man with long, stringy, brown hair answered the door. George told the Big Dog what we wanted. The Big Dog stood there in his torn jeans and green army jacket.

"C'mon in for a minute," he said. "Yeah, I can get you some wine, but we'll have to drive to DeTour to buy it."

Big Dog disappeared behind the curtain separating his bedroom from the main room. He re-emerged carrying a red flag, then holding it up by the corners. "This is a North Vietnamese flag I got off a dead gook," he said. "This was the only thing those bastards let me leave the country with. I had a necklace of ears they took away from me before they'd let me on the plane to come back."

Oh, no. I was getting a bad feeling.

"That place was full of people trying to tell you how you should do shit. There was this one big sergeant that was the worst. Thought he was the meanest, baddest man in country. It didn't take long before I fragged his black ass and ended that problem."

This was getting worse.

"We'll take my car," Big Dog said.

We walked down the concrete block steps and got into Big Dog's car, a two-door, light blue Camaro. I climbed into the back seat while Al settled into the passenger bucket seat.

Big Dog hit the starter and the engine roared to life. He gunned it. His lips stretched over his teeth as he grinned. "302 cubic inches, 290 horsepower, Holley carb, and four-on-the-floor," he chortled as he dropped it in gear and threw gravel as we exited his driveway onto the highway. There he squealed the tires after shifting into second gear, and then again as he hit third gear.

The speed limit was sixty-five mile per hour. A quarter-mile down the highway, we were doing seventy-five when I sneaked a peek at the speedometer from the back seat. Twilight in Upper

Michigan was a dangerous time to travel highways at high speeds because that's when the white-tail deer gathered on roadsides to feed on grass.

"This baby goes so fast they gotta consider giving me a ticket for flying too low," Big Dog laughed.

We flew down M-134, also known as the Scenic Highway, as it paralleled the Lake Huron shoreline between Cedarville and DeTour. Then Big Dog tromped the gas pedal. Eight-five miles per hour. Ninety-five miles per hour. One hundred miles per hour! Then one hundred ten, one hundred twenty! I had never gone that fast before. I'd never been in a car that would go one hundred miles per hour. At that speed, the highway wasn't very scenic.

Glances out the side window looking toward the woods revealed nothing but a green blur; out the other side, just gray water with occasional green blips as we ripped past clumps of trees at the water's edge.

We were going to hit a deer and die. I knew it. There in the back seat, I was taking stock of the situation. I made promises I knew I could never keep to a God whose very existence I questioned.

When we hit DeTour village limits, Big Dog brought the car down to a respectable town speed and pulled into a store parking lot. He got out and came back a couple minutes later with two brown paper bags. He handed our bottle of Mogen David Blackberry wine to Al. The package he had purchased with our extra cash was tucked under the driver's seat. "Four on the floor and a fifth under the seat," he snickered, as though we had never heard that one before.

Big Dog backed out of the parking lot, and we headed back

to Cedarville in the near dark. I don't know why, but Big Dog kept the speed down to seventy-five miles per hour, way faster than I ever drove, especially at night, but it wasn't as heart-stopping as one hundred miles per hour, either.

I never asked Al to ask Big Dog to buy alcohol for us ever again.

The Big Dog was out of my life until a year later, when he stepped onto the deck of the Club ferry.

The Les Cheneaux Club was an association of wealthy people who had summer homes, "cottages" they called them, on both sides of the Club Point on Marquette Island. Ownership of those homes was strictly regulated by the association.

The only access to the island was by boat. Through their annual dues, the Club paid for the operation and maintenance of a ferry as well as a maintenance crew for the buildings and common areas owned by the association.

My summer job for three years while going to college was to run a ferry carrying freight and passengers over the half-mile run between the Club Dock at the Les Cheneaux Golf Course on the mainland and the Club Dock on Marquette Island. I picked up workers from the mainland at 7:30 a.m. (before the workday began at 8:00 a.m.) and ferried workers back to the mainland when the workday ended at 4:30 p.m. For that, I was paid for nine hours per day, six days per week. On Sundays, I worked only eight hours, 8:00 a.m. to 4:30 p.m., with a half-hour lunch.

The wooden boat was twenty-five feet long, built locally, and modeled after a Maine lobster boat. Its hull was gray and had a white cabin with internal steering controls and bench seating for customers choosing to ride out of the weather. For

the most part, I ran the boat from the port (left) side of the aft
deck with a steering board hooked to the steering cables rather
than a wheel. I pushed forward on the lever to turn right; pulled
back on the lever to turn left. I held the steering lever in place
with my butt, leaving both hands to manipulate the throttle and
gear controls mounted on the back side of the cabin. A vertical
post with an iron crosspiece mounted on the back deck was used
to hook tow lines for the barges loaded with salt for the water
softener, LP gas tanks, or barrels of fuel oil. Swinging a barge at
the end of a tow line, so it gently bumped up against the dock
rather than crashing into it and causing property damage, was a
skill I developed.

In a small notebook, I recorded the number of passengers
I ferried back and forth and to which of the Club members
their passage would be charged. The charge was a dollar for each
passenger and fifty cents for a bag of groceries. Dick Smith, the
resident caretaker, and work supervisor for the Club, told me
to keep the notebook hidden beneath a cushion in the boat's
cabin. Apparently, charging passengers made the ferry a commercial vessel requiring a Coast Guard-licensed pilot. I was eighteen,
just out of high school. I had no license.

Depending on the boat traffic in the channel, it took ten
minutes to run the half-mile between the mainland and the
island. The ferry put out quite the wake that during periods
of high water on the Great Lakes would inundate the channel's crib docks. There were large bells mounted on dark green
wooden cradles on each of the ferry docks, bells so loud and
resonant that they would have been appropriate in church bell
towers. People that needed the ferry on one side or the other
would rock the bell in the cradle, allowing the clapper to strike it

several times. That would be the signal for me to leave the dock for the other side. They would also ring the bell on the mainland side if I was needed to fuel up their boats at the dockside gas pump.

I formed an intense dislike for a couple of the teenaged kids who seemed to run their outboards low on gas every day, speeding through the channels the Les Cheneaux were reportedly named after.

"Gas! Gas!" they screamed as they raced at full throttle past the docked ferry on the Marquette Island side. If I wasn't fast enough, they'd tie up at the gas pump and start ringing the bell. Damn, I grew to hate that bell.

One Monday morning, the Big Dog was waiting his turn to jump on the ferry for a ride to the island. He didn't recognize me, but I certainly recognized him. It turned out that the Big Dog was working with a crew for a construction contractor who had a job on the island. Each day, Big Dog boarded the ferry at 7:30 in the morning to go to the island. I returned him to the mainland every afternoon at 4:30.

On a sunny Friday at noon, I had tied up the ferry on the mainland side. I walked up the dock to the clubhouse at the golf course. There I wrestled a bottle of Royal Crown Cola out of the old vending machine and bought a bag of Made Rite potato chips to supplement my lunch of three peanut butter and jelly sandwiches and hot tea.

I was sitting on the ferry finishing up lunch when two men pulled into the dock in a sixteen-foot aluminum outboard boat. They wore dark suits, white shirts, and black ties. I had never seen anybody operating an outboard in coats and ties before. They both sported dark glasses. They tied up and approached the ferry. Neither was carrying a Bible, so it was unlikely they were Jehovah's Witnesses.

Thinking they wanted a ride, I exited the cabin and stood on the deck.

"I'm Agent Prescott, FBI," the taller man, "and this," nodding toward his partner, "is Agent Ralston. We need some information," he continued as he pulled a leather folder from his jacket and flipped it open.

I just caught sight of a shiny badge and an identification card before Agent Prescott flipped it closed. He tucked it back in his inner jacket pocket.

Oh, geez. Had I tucked the ferry logbook out of sight the last time I entered a charge? I didn't dare look back into the cabin to make sure it was tucked all the way under the cushion. Were they going to arrest me for operating a vessel without a license?

"What do you do with this boat?" Agent Prescott continued.

Swallowing hard, I said, "I run the Club crew to Marquette Island in the morning and back again at the end of the day." Then I added, "If there's any groceries delivered to the dock during the day, I haul them over, too."

Agent Prescott pulled a notebook and pen from his other inner jacket pocket and wrote that down.

"Were you working this morning?"

"Yes, sir." Agent Prescott made a note.

"Did you transport James Leavitt to the island on this boat this morning?"

Screwing up my face and pursing my lips, I thought. There wasn't any James Leavitt on the Club crew.

Agent Prescott added, "You might know him as ... Big Dog."

"Yes, sir," I said, getting a real bad feeling. "I took him over to the island this morning, just before 8:00 o'clock."

Agent Prescott wrote that down.

"Did you bring him back to the mainland today?" he asked.

"No, sir!" I insisted.

"Have you taken anybody off the island today?" he asked pointedly.

"No, sir! Nobody has come back across ... all day today!"

Agent Prescott wrote that down. Meanwhile, Agent Ralston walked to the bow of the ferry and peered through the windows. I thought about the logbook.

"Is there any way off this island other than by boat?"

"No, sir" I said, turning my attention back to Agent Prescott.

Agent Prescott made a final note on his pad and returned it to his jacket.

He looked at me. "This boat does not leave this dock until I tell you it can leave."

"Yes, sir," was my shaky reply.

The FBI agents returned to their boat, untied it, and sped up the channel to Marquette Island.

When they were out of sight, I ducked into the boat cabin. The corner of the logbook was exposed. Grimacing, I tucked it further under a cushion deeper in the cabin.

Well. The FBI had told me the ferry couldn't go anywhere. I went back up to the golf course clubhouse, dropped a dime in the old vending machine, and wrestled out another bottle of RC

Cola.

When the bell began a plaintive peal on the Club dock on the island side, I smiled. I sauntered on down to the ferry, where I sat on the gunwale to sip my RC Cola in the heat. I peered up the channel to the bell on the other side and could make out one person in a short-sleeved white shirt standing next to the dark green bell cradle.

It had to be Dick Smith, my supervisor, and the caretaker for the Club. I grinned. Then I waved, not because he could see me, but because it felt good to ignore the bell. After all, I was under orders from the FBI.

When Dick didn't see the ferry pull out from the dock, he rang the bell again, not once or twice, but an insistent five or six times. I stood firm.

Dick waited for a short time, the amount of time it would have taken me to run from the golf course clubhouse down to the ferry. When it was apparent the ferry wasn't starting up, he rang the bell again. An angry series of peals coursed up and down the channel alerting people from the neighboring town of Hessel and a phalanx of tightly-packed waterfront summer homes in both directions that *someone* was pretty damned unhappy with the performance of the Les Cheneaux Club ferry operator!

Finally, the bell quit ringing. A minute later, I saw a small aluminum outboard pull out from one of the docks adjacent to the Club dock on Marquette Island. At the outboard tiller was a man in a short-sleeved white shirt. I mentally rehearsed what I would say. Should I cut him off as soon as I saw him by announcing that I was under direct orders of the FBI? Or should I wait and let him vent his anger first? It was delicious.

It took Dick less than five minutes to reach me in his borrowed outboard. He pulled into the dock behind the ferry so fast I thought he might swamp the little boat. I stood on the pier, intending to grab his bow line to help him tie-up. He grabbed a line on his side of the transom, scrambled onto the dock, and threw a quick clove hitch over the cedar piling. I reached down to pick up his bow line, and clove hitched it to a piling as well.

He was hollering as soon as he stepped onto the dock.

"What the hell are you doing? Didn't you hear me ringing the bell? What the hell's wrong with you?"

"Geez, Dick," I said apologetically. I had decided to let him vent first. "The FBI told me that I couldn't move the ferry until they told me it was OK."

"What!? The FBI?!"

"Yeah," I said. "Those guys." I pointed up the channel toward the Club dock. The men in dark suits and white shirts were just about to land their little boat back at our dock. "They were looking for the Big Dog and told me I couldn't take anybody off the island until they gave me the okay."

Dick hurried over to the spot where the FBI guys were landing their boat. Dick took the bow line they handed him and helped tie the boat to the dock. They conferred, just out of earshot. Dick nodded several times, shook his head once. He started back in my direction and then turned.

Pointing at me, he said to the FBI men, "He can run the ferry now, can't he?" Agent Prescott nodded.

The Big Dog had eluded Agents Prescott and Ralston that day. I heard rumors that the FBI was watching his house all day. Neighbors who knew Big Dog and who he worked for had called the island and alerted him. Apparently, Big Dog had convinced a young woman who worked for a family on the island to give him a ride over to the mainland in one of the family's small outboard boats.

Why did the FBI want him? Did it have anything to do with the fragging incident from the war he bragged about? I didn't think the FBI would have any interest in apprehending some guy who bought kids bottles of Mogen David Blackberry wine.

I never saw, heard of, or spoke of the Big Dog again. Until thirty-five years later when I crossed paths with Dan.

You'll Never Take Me Alive

I GREW UP IN MICHIGAN. You might recall from your geography classes that Michigan is in the middle on top of the continental United States. It's the state that's shaped like a mitten. But there are two parts to the state. The mitten part is the Lower Peninsula. I grew up in the Upper Peninsula, the part that arches over top of the Lower. There are some differences between the two parts of the state. The Upper Peninsula (the U.P. to locals, who call themselves *Yoopers*) is relatively undeveloped with lots of forests and swamps with few roads, while the Lower Peninsula is Detroit, Grand Rapids, Flint, and Lansing. South of the bridge, there were more factories and more roads than you can count. Folks that lived "Down Below" considered those of us in the U.P. as somewhat backward and unsophisticated.

My parents were hardworking folks. Dad worked seasonally in construction. He fixed cars, lawnmowers—anything with an engine—out in the garage in the winter. He built cabinets, furniture, and houses. Mom worked at the two grocery stores in town. She'd worked as a teller at our local bank branch and went on to edit our weekly newspaper for many years. They had raised my sister and me to respect authority, respect teachers, and respect our elders.

By the time I graduated high school, I pretty much knew everything. I went on to college to fill in a few knowledge gaps. Man, I had the world by the ass in a downhill drag. In 1973, I was between my junior and senior years in college. I needed a car to accept a summer job with the US Forest Service in Lower Michigan. I did buy a car, a blue 1970 Plymouth Belvedere with a black vinyl roof and a 318 cubic-inch engine. We put it in my mother's name because, despite the fact I knew everything, insurance companies didn't have much faith in a twenty-one-year-old and his driving abilities. Putting ownership of the car in Mom's name gave us a break on insurance rates.

One Friday afternoon that fall, I came home from school for the weekend and found my mother sitting at the kitchen table, tapping an envelope into the palm of her hand like a beat cop might do with his baton. The envelope had a big seal on it like it might be important.

"Have you ever been to Lansing?" she asked, getting right to the point. There was no "Hi, how are you doing? How did school go this week?"

Puzzled, I answered, "No, I've never been to Lansing."

"Never loaned your car to someone who drove it to Lansing?"

"Absolutely not," I said. "Nobody but me drives my car."

"Well, how do you explain this?" she asked, handing me the envelope. Inside was a letter with an official-looking letterhead.

Dear Mrs. Griffin:

In August of this year, your vehicle was cited for a parking violation in the City of Lansing. You failed to take advantage of the opportunity to pay your fine by mail within the time limit described in your citation.

We have set a date in December to bring your case before a judge. Your appearance in court is mandatory. Should you fail to appear, a bench warrant will be issued for your arrest.

Your attention to this matter would be greatly appreciated.

Sincerely,

Roger Harris

Assistant Attorney
City of Lansing

By the grim look on her face, I knew she was taking this seriously.

"Geez, Mom! I've never been to Lansing. My car has never been to Lansing! I don't know how this happened."

Mom gave me a look, you know the one, the "lie detector look," the stare that all mothers have. From experience, that look was about 99 percent effective. I passed the test. She believed me. The next day she handed me a letter she typed in response.

Dear Mr. Harris:

Just where do you get off frightening little old ladies from the Upper Peninsula half to death with mandatory court appearances and threats of arrest warrants for parking violations?

For your information, neither my car nor my son, who drives my car, has ever been to Lansing. I believe a mistake has been made. I suggest that you double-check your records before pursuing this further.

Your attention to this matter would be greatly appreciated.

Sincerely,

Aldyth Griffin
Mother of Two
Town of Cedarville

"Holy smokes," I said, handing the letter back to her, "isn't this just asking for more trouble?"

"Maybe," she said, "but I want them to know I'm serious." She looked at her letter again, frowning.

"It's still missing something," she said.

She picked up her BIC pen and wrote across the bottom of the page in big, bold, block letters:

P.S. YOU'LL NEVER TAKE ME ALIVE!

She folded her letter, slipped it into the envelope, and licked the adhesive flap before sealing it.

Three weeks later she received another official-looking letter from the City of Lansing.

Dear Mrs. Griffin:

We really don't like frightening little old ladies from the U.P. half to death. For the most part, it's far too cold and way too dark up there for our comfort.

At your suggestion, we did review our records regarding this citation. Lo and behold, a mistake HAD been made. While the license plate number was correct, we found that the vehicle in question was registered in the State of New Mexico, rather than the State of Michigan!

Please accept my deepest apologies for causing you and your family any distress in this matter.

Sincerely,

Roger Harris
Assistant Attorney
City of Lansing

At the bottom of the letter was a hand-written note, printed in neat block letters:

> P.S. Had it come down to executing a warrant for your arrest, I would like to think we could have avoided bloodshed. As of 1937, the City of Lansing no longer hangs parking violators.

Mom and Dad are both gone now, but they left my sister and me with a wonderful inheritance, not the kind of inheritance that would allow us to go out and buy a new truck or a new boat but the kind of inheritance that will last us the rest of our lives: values of respect for people in authority, respect for teachers, respect for our elders, and the idea that maybe, just maybe, a little humor even in serious circumstances can help you out of a pinch. Thanks, Mom.

He's My Brother

WITHIN WALKING DISTANCE OF MY HOME on the Four Mile Block, southeast of Cedarville, there was a neighborhood bar. One family had owned the Snows Bar for years. The Snows Bar was where I had spent the first money I'd ever earned on my own. In the summer of 1967, I mowed grass at summer homes on the Snows Channel. I pushed my lawn mower a half-mile down the street one day and mowed three lawns. Each owner had paid me one dollar and twenty-five cents. As I pushed my mower past the Snows on my way home, that newly earned money cried out to be spent. I walked into the bar and bought myself six bottles of Coke right out of the cooler and drank one as I pushed the mower the rest of the way home.

Friday and Saturday nights usually found the gravel parking lot full at The Snows. Almost always, two or three cars were parked in front of the bar at any time of day. Area folks often stopped by for a glass of beer and the locally famous, hand-crafted "Snows Burger."

It was a small bar with vertical board-and-batten siding painted white. A smaller addition off to the left housed the grill that had been added years before when the owner decided to offer a limited menu. In the front, steps led to a storm door to an enclosed porch where a customer could shake off the rain or stomp the snow from his boots before entering. The owner greeted local customers by name from behind the varnished bar.

The barroom was filled with rustic cedar tables and chairs darkened by years of smoke and layers of varnish. There was a small dance floor off to the right, a place where my grand-mother, Ione Steel, sometimes played organ music for weekend crowds. She had a fancy organ that had tabs for percussion rhythm and string chords to accompany her organ playing. She could really get the crowd going with her renditions of the "Beer Barrel Polka" and "Too Fat Polka," among other favorites. A pool table to the left of the entry completed the interior.

After achieving adulthood, or at least achieving the legal drinking age in Michigan, I enjoyed walking down to the Snows, seating myself at the bar, drinking a couple of draft beers at a dime apiece, and shooting a game of pool or two at a quarter a game. For a buck, I could have five glasses of beer and shoot at least two games of pool, maybe more if I were lucky enough to beat an opponent and get him to pay for another game.

I remember one hot summer day in 1973 in particular. I had finished up my workday piloting the Club ferry carrying work crews and freight between the mainland and their job sites on Marquette Island. After work, I walked down to the Snows for a cold beer. When I walked in, I observed a couple of regu-lars seated at the far end of the bar, engaged in quiet debate. They passed a bar napkin and a pen back and forth, obviously making notes or adding lines to a complex figure.

I sat at the corner of the bar nearest the pool table and asked the bartender for a Stroh's draft beer. While waiting, I slid off my barstool, put a quarter in the pool table's slot, and began playing a game against myself. As I was sizing up the final shot to sink the eight ball and win the game, a stranger walked in and took a stool a couple seats from my own.

He was about my size with wavy light brown, almost blond hair, maybe five or ten years older than me. He looked vaguely familiar, as though I should know him from somewhere. He paid for a draft beer and turned to watch me at the pool table.

I lined up my shot on the eight ball. I missed. I took another turn, this time as my opponent and missed that shot as well. I line up another shot on the eight ball and finally sank it.

The familiar-looking stranger at the bar stepped down from his stool and pulled a quarter from his pocket. "Are you up for a game?" he asked. He smiled and the smile lines deepened from the edge of his nose to the corners of his mouth.

"Sure thing," I replied.

"I'm Dana," he said.

"Pete."

When he smiled, his laugh lines became more prominent, extending from the edge of his nose to each corner of his mouth.

Money breaks, so I racked the balls. Dana sank a ball off the opening break, lined up another, sank that, but missed his third shot. I made an easy shot, missed the next. He dropped two more. It was apparent I was outclassed.

On my next shot, the cue ball was hemmed. There was only one direct path to even hit one of my balls, and then I would have to bank that off the far rail to sink it in the corner pocket. I looked the table over, tried to figure out where to hit the cue ball and where to hit the ball I wanted to bank in, and where I had to bounce it off the rail on the far side of the table.

After watching me for a minute trying to figure out my shot, Dana interrupted my concentration. He said he found it helpful to use the diamonds on the rails to line up shots. He explained the technique I'd never heard of before. Following his instructions, I made the bank shot, much to my surprise. I lost the game, but I put up another quarter, and we played another game while sipping our cold Stroh's.

Dana had grown up in the Cedarville area but moved away early in life. He was back in town visiting his mother, Mary Allen. I knew her as she used to sign us up for unemployment checks once a week at the town hall during the fall and winter. Each week, when we picked up our check, we had to affirm that we were looking and available for work. One week, I told Mary that I would be unavailable the next week as I would visit my grandfather in Central America.

"Who is your grandfather?" she asked.

"John Steel," I responded.

"Oh!" she said, surprised. Then she smiled. "I know him."

Dana and I finished our pool games, drained our glasses, and parted ways.

"Nice talking to you," I said in parting.

"Nice talking to you, too," he replied.

We left the bar and walked out of the parking lot. When we reached the street, Dana turned left. I turned right.

The next morning at breakfast, I told Mom about the guy I'd met at the bar the night before. "Nice guy," I said. "And I know his mother, Mary, from picking up my unemployment check."

"I feel like I should know him. He looked so familiar," I

added.

Mom glanced down at the table, sighed, and then looked me in the eye.

"He's my brother," she said.

"What!?"

"My father and Mary had an affair after the war. Dana was the result."

That was it. Dana looked like a younger version of my mother's brother, Uncle John. Dana had the Steel look, the smile lines, the blond hair that grew in waves on top of his head. Dana looked like my grandfather in photographs from his younger years.

I dearly loved my grandfather, but learned that he had cheated on my grandmother. I wondered if that was what led to their eventual divorce in the late 1950s.

Dana and I never crossed paths again.

Many years later, I thought about Dana and tried to find information about him on the internet. I figured it might be time to have a conversation, however delicate. I wondered if he knew or suspected the truth of his heritage. I wondered if Dana's children knew. But that was none of my business.

I never tried to contact him or his family, thinking I would be angry if approached by a stranger who claimed my father was not my biological father. "Just let it be," I thought to myself.

I found Dana's obituary from 2015. Dana had left Cedarville for Florida with his parents after their resort was destroyed by fire when he was very young. He joined the army in 1968 and served until 1972, when he returned home. By then, his mother, Mary, was living in Cedarville. I imagine that was about the time I met Dana in the Snows Bar.

The obituary went on to say Dana "was outgoing and enjoyed visiting with people about almost any subject." I could attest to that. There was no mention of relatives other than his parents, his siblings, and his children.

I still wonder.

Let's Go Fishing

IN THE SPRING OF 1973, I WAS A JUNIOR at Lake Superior State College and looking for summer work. The college placement service wasn't much help. On the other hand, my mother had seen a notice that the Financial Aid Department had some opportunities through the college Work-Study Program. I talked to the folks in financial aid and took an application.

I discovered that I could apply for work-study jobs with the US Forest Service all around the country. What caught my eye immediately were jobs with Wilderness trail crews in the Boundary Waters Canoe Area in Minnesota or on the Misty Fjords National Monument in Alaska! I had three choices, but I didn't bother to add a third choice.

In May, I received a letter accepting me into the work-study program and offering placement into a position as a biological aide on the Huron-Manistee National Forest. Huron-Manistee?

That was a national forest in Lower Michigan! I didn't realize there was a national forest there. I guessed it wasn't all roads, cities, and suburbs below the Mackinac Bridge. I accepted the job offer though I was a bit disappointed at not having been selected for either of my only two choices.

The job was located at Huron-Manistee headquarters in the town of Cadillac, 200 miles from home. It paid more per hour than my last job running the Club Ferry, but it was limited to forty hours per week, whereas the ferry's job was sixty-two hours per week. I figured I could save money by living in a tent in a National Forest campground for the summer rather than renting an apartment.

I left home on a Friday morning for the job that would begin Monday morning. For the first time in my life, I was going to be on my own. I crossed the Mackinac Bridge headed south, crossing the bridge by myself for the first time ever. It felt good.

I had my Michigan road map which showed a fairly direct route to Cadillac. Somewhere along the line, I followed signs detouring me around a highway construction zone. I missed the sign that would have gotten me back on the right road.

I ended up on gravel and sand back roads with no road signs other than Forest Service road numbers, which are *not* shown on State of Michigan road maps. After a couple of hours, taking one turn after another, I realized that I needed to drive in one direction until I came to a paved highway and then on to a town identified on a map.

Eventually, I pulled into Cadillac late in the afternoon. Locating Forest Service headquarters, I reported in for work. Then I found a Forest Service campground where I could set up my tent camper.

But the best part was when I arrived at that campground, I found that there were two women from Lake Superior State College doing the same thing: working for the Forest Service for the summer and sharing a tent in the same campground.

Well, over the course of the summer, Kathy, Laurie, and I became good friends. Truth be told, I developed strong feelings of affection for Kathy, a tall, dark-haired beauty, not that she was ever going to know how I felt. I was a terribly shy and socially awkward young man.

Later that summer, Kathy's parents, Bill and Marge, visited, driving four or five hours from Detroit to the camp-ground. Bill was a formidable figure of a man. He stood six-foot-four inches tall and was a pipefitter by trade. His musculature reflected his life of hard work. Kathy's mother, Marge, on the other hand, stood only five-foot-six, but she was from Pennsylvania coal country and was no less imposing. Introductions were made. When Kathy's folks learned who I was, they stood on either side of me and began firing questions at me, one after the other. I'd blurt out an answer to one, and the other would immediately hit me with the next interrogatory.

Bill: "What does your father do for a living?"

Marge: "Does your mother work, or is she at home?"

Bill: "What kind of a truck does he drive, Ford or Chevy ... or *Dodge?*"

Marge: "When are you going to graduate?"

Bill: "What kind of a job can you get with a degree in... *biology?*"

This questioning dragged on for well, several minutes. I broke into a sweat.

After they'd left for home on Sunday, I told Kathy that her folks had really put me through an interrogation.

She laughed. "It could have been worse," she said. "I didn't tell them you were my boyfriend."

Boyfriend? I had a girlfriend! If you've ever been a young

man, you might remember a time in your life when that might have been the most dazzling realization in the world!

As my luck would have it, Kathy and I were married two years later. Bill and Marge would come to visit their daughter. I was never really sure how, or even if, I fit into that family. Sometimes I felt like I was the stranger who had stolen their oldest daughter.

Eventually, my job with the Forest Service took Kathy and me, and the kids by then, to the Chippewa National Forest on the shores of beautiful Leech Lake in Northern Minnesota. Bill and Marge came to visit Kathy and the kids there.

On one trip, Marge mentioned that she had noticed a new boat parked in the driveway.

"Oh, yeah," I said. "Brand new fourteen foot Lund, solid aluminum, 25 horse Johnson motor. The walleye fishing here is great!"

"Walleyes," Marge said. "Walleyes are my favorite fish, certainly the best eating." She gave me a long appraising look. "Let's go fishing," she said.

So, we went out fishing walleyes the next morning. We did well that day and again the next day. On our third morning out, we'd just started fishing when Marge gave me another one of those appraising looks. "My sister Ann and I used to fish together all the time in Montana before she passed away last year. We had an ongoing bet: twenty-five cents for the first fish, twenty-five cents for the biggest fish, and twenty-five cents for the most fish. Would you be interested in taking me up on that bet?"

Would I? Here was a chance for me to win seventy-five cents every day I took my mother-in-law out fishing. "Certainly,"

I said.

Within moments. "Hey, Marge, first fish!" I said, pulling one into the boat.

She looked at it. "That's not a walleye. That's a perch. We're fishing for walleyes. Perch don't count."

Oh, OK. "Hey Marge, first walleye," I said, pulling a walleye into the boat.

"That's awfully small," she said. "We haven't kept any that small before. Doesn't count."

Huh. Apparently, there were some rules to this betting game with which I was not entirely familiar, especially Rule Number One, *Marge makes the rules.*

Eventually, I learned almost all the rules, and every fishing trip after that ended up in us exchanging quarters.

Despite Marge's invitation to participate in her betting game, I was not yet aware of just how seriously Marge took her fishing. I would learn one morning out on Leech Lake. It was a good day of fishing. Marge had five walleyes, but I had only caught three.

About mid-morning, Marge started fidgeting and squirming around on her boat seat. Finally, she couldn't take it anymore. "I saw a bathroom at the boat landing. We have to go in right now."

"But ... " I said.

"Right now," she said.

Luckily, the boat landing was only five minutes away, so we pulled up our gear and headed back to the landing. Before the boat had even bumped into the dock, Marge was up and out of her seat, springing from the boat onto the dock like a cat. She immediately headed toward the bathroom in the parking lot. I was in awe. I'd never seen her move as gracefully or as fast.

Surprised, I grabbed the dock to steady the boat and reached for the lines to tie up. Glancing toward the parking lot, I saw that Marge had stopped. She was talking to a stranger before resuming her dash. I tied up the boat and was arranging the fishing gear when the stranger Marge had talked to sauntered down to the dock.

He stood there on the dock, looking down at me, hands in pockets. "So, the word on the street is that your mother-in-law out fished you this morning."

Was Marge competitive? The only thing that could stop her on her quest to find a bathroom was the opportunity to stop and brag to a perfect stranger that she had out fished her son-in-law.

A few years later, Kathy, the kids, and I transferred to the Tongass National Forest in Ketchikan, Alaska. Bill and Marge came to visit.

On their first visit, Marge said, "I hear the fishing in Alaska is really good. What do you fish for this time of year?"

"Oh, gosh, the kings are in. They're the biggest and the best eating of all the salmon. You can grill them, bake them, and smoked king salmon might be the best fish you ever tasted. They usually run fifteen, twenty-five pounds, and sometimes even bigger."

"Let's go fishing," she said.

The next morning, Marge and I went fishing for king salmon.

Now, fishing for king salmon wasn't like fishing for wall-eyes. With walleyes, you caught a bunch in one morning. I'd warned Marge that a guy had to fish an average of thirty hours before catching a king, and that was when they were biting. I didn't have high hopes.

We trolled for an hour. No bites. After two hours, we'd pretty much run out of conversation. After three hours, I'd run out of coffee. At four hours, I was about out of patience and about to suggest we call it a morning and head back home for lunch. But before I had a chance to say it out loud, Marge's fishing rod bent over double, and the drag was screaming as line jerked off the reel.

"Marge! You've got a fish! Set the hook!"

She picked up her rod and heaved back on it. The fish felt the hook bite in, and it began running, steadily pulling line off the level-wind reel. Marge was frantically cranking even as the mighty fish was pulling line out.

"No, Marge! Pump and reel. Put your thumb on the reel to slow the fish down and then pump it back toward you, then reel the rod tip down! Pump and reel."

She tried that and started making headway. The fish would run twenty feet, and she would bring it back twenty-five. The fish would run forty feet, and she would bring it back thirty-five. After twenty minutes, she had gained on it, but when the fish got close, it saw the boat and took off on a long run. "Zzzzz," the drag on the reel screamed! That fish took fifty feet of line! "Zzzz," and seventy-five feet of line were gone. "Zzzz," and now one hundred feet had been stripped off the reel. Still, that fish ran.

Suddenly the line drooped and went slack. Marge's shoulders slumped. She looked at the rod, looked at me. "It's gone," she said in a plaintive voice.

I looked out in the general direction of that fish's last

known location. It looked like a scene from *Jaws*: dorsal fin sticking up out of the water, a wave being pushed in front of its nose. "No, he's not, Marge!" I yelled. "He's heading for the boat! Reel as fast as you can!"

She reeled in the slack line as fast as she could, eventually catching up with the fish. When it felt the pull on the line again, it went straight down, a hundred feet. Marge held on to the pulsing rod as the fish stripped line from the reel. She stopped it, or the fish hit bottom, and she began pumping and reeling, pulling that fish back up from the depths of the green waters.

It took another fifteen minutes, but she finally had the fish exhausted, laying on the surface on its side about six feet from the boat. I could see there was only one hook in it, barely in the corner of its mouth. One more run, and that fish really would be gone. "Bring it closer, Marge, so I can net it!"

I glanced over and saw Marge was about as exhausted as that fish. She was so tired, she couldn't raise her fishing rod with the flasher and trolling lead above her waist. I thought about grabbing her line to pull the fish within net range, but one thing I'd learned over the years fishing with Marge was: YOU DO NOT TOUCH HER FISHING LINE.

I did the next best thing that came to mind. I grabbed the landing net by the very end of the handle. I hooked my heels under my seat and lunged over the side of the boat as far as I could reach, bruising my ribs on the gunwale (oh, that hurt). Concentrating, I slipped the net under the fish and raised it. The fish was in the net!

I pulled the net to the boat, reached over the side, and bunched the net over the fish so it couldn't flop out, and hoisted it in, dropping it on the floorboards between us.

We sat exhausted and just stared at it: thirty-seven pounds of quivering, ice cold, wild Alaska king salmon!

I stepped over the fish to give Marge the hearty Minnesota fishing guide handshake, and the "beautiful fish, good job" line.

Well, she set her fishing rod down, put a hand on each of my shoulders, stood on her tippy toes, and gave me a kiss. Right. On. The. Lips.

There was no doubt about it. I was now *in* with my wife's family!

According to Kathy, Marge catching that fish marked an obvious turning point in our relationship. Prior to landing that king salmon, Marge's first questions to Kathy when she called were about how she and the kids were doing. After that king salmon, Marge's first questions were: "Has Pete been fishing?" followed by "What did he catch?"

Bill and Marge visited Alaska every year. Marge and I spent every day possible out fishing. Some days Bill went with us. We caught king salmon. We caught silvers. We pulled halibut off the bottom in 300 feet of water.

When Bill got sick, Marge stayed at home for several years to take care of him.

After Bill passed away, Marge decided to come back to Alaska on her own, and we took up where we'd left off. We caught king salmon. We caught silvers. We caught halibut. We watched groups of humpback whales feeding on schools of herring. We watched brown bears with their cubs feeding along the shoreline. One day killer whales surrounded our boat, staring at us as much as we stared at them.

When Marge's hips started giving her problems, she couldn't walk up and down the ramp to and from the boat. We rented a wheelchair. I would wheel her down to the boat at the start of the day and wheel her back up to the parking lot at the end of the day's fishing. We must have been quite the sight, out on our favorite fishing spots with a wheelchair lashed to the top of the boat.

Eventually, age and infirmity caught up with Marge, and she became too frail to travel. Our fishing adventures together did finally come to an end.

Marge passed away in February 2008.

For the life of me, I can't remember the last king salmon she ever caught. But I'll never forget her first.

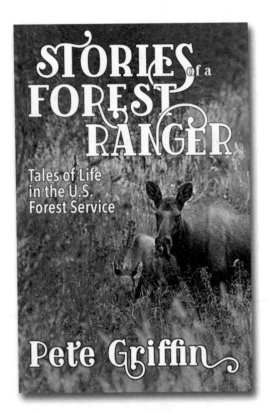

Published 2020
Paperback • $14.95
978-1-62491-157-6
208 Pages @ 5.5" x 8.5"
E-book • $10.99
978-1-62491-158-3
Adult & YA

Musings of a wildlife biologist

"Griffin's voice is full of wonder and wisdom that only comes from thinking deeply about the natural world, and about human nature. His voice, both personal and unique, rings through these stories, clear and crisp as a winter morning."

–Steve Daut, President of the Ann Arbor Storytellers Guild and author of *Telling Twain*

Pete Griffin grew up in the pristine woodlands of northern Michigan, studied forestry and biology in college,and served the US Forest Service his entire career. In semi-retirement, he has become a professional storyteller working on Disney and Princess cruises along the Alaskan coast. Griffin lives with his wife in Juno, Alaska. This is his first book.

"Griffin masterfully captures the essence of living and working in the woods. He brings the story of his career to life by sharing reflections on the majesty of our national parks, lessons learned, fishes landed, and the family that is our National Forest Service. His easy storytelling style makes these humorous and touching encounters with wolves, eagles, skunks and other wildlife hard to put down."

   –Jeff Doyle, storyteller/humorist

"Like a braided stream that crosses and re-crosses a main channel, Pete Griffin's Stories of a Forest Ranger take his readers into the woods of a Michigan childhood filled with curiosity and wonder then carry them along as his professional life and way of seeing and learning unfold. Our guide has the keen eye of a naturalist, the discerning objectivity of a scientist, and the voice of an accomplished storyteller and raconteur. Always ready to reinterpret lessons learned and apply to both his personal and professional life, Pete's stories are salted with dry humor, and seasoned with a whole lot of heart.

"Life is full of doors," he tell young people. "Don't be afraid to go through them and find out what's on the other side." Open the door to Stories of a Forest Ranger and you're sure to enjoy what you find inside!"

   –Bob Kanegis, author and professional storyteller

If you have enjoyed these stories, point your browser to:

www.thestorytellingranger.com

www.parkhursbrothers.com

www.storynet.org